Connecting Sch
Multilingual Home

NEW PERSPECTIVES ON LANGUAGE AND EDUCATION
Founding Editor: Viv Edwards, *University of Reading, UK*

Series Editors: Phan Le Ha, *University of Hawaii at Manoa, USA* and Joel Windle, *Monash University, Australia.*

Two decades of research and development in language and literacy education have yielded a broad, multidisciplinary focus. Yet education systems face constant economic and technological change, with attendant issues of identity and power, community and culture. This series will feature critical and interpretive, disciplinary and multidisciplinary perspectives on teaching and learning, language and literacy in new times.

All books in this series are externally peer-reviewed.

Full details of all the books in this series and of all our other publicati~ can be found on http://www.multilingual-matters.com, or by w Multilingual Matters, St Nicholas House, 31–34 High Street, I 2AW, UK.

NEW PERSPECTIVES ON LANGUAGE AND EDUCATION: 69
Ideas and Reflections in Practice

Connecting School and the Multilingual Home

Theory and Practice for Rural Educators

Maria R. Coady

MULTILINGUAL MATTERS
Bristol • Blue Ridge Summit

DOI https://doi.org/10.21832/COADY3262
Library of Congress Cataloging in Publication Data
A catalog record for this book is available from the Library of Congress.
Names: Coady, Maria R., author.
Title: Connecting School and the Multilingual Home: Theory and Practice for Rural Educators/Maria R. Coady.
Description: Blue Ridge Summit, PA: Multilingual Matters, [2019] | Series: New Perspectives on Language and Education: 69 | Includes bibliographical references and index.
Identifiers: LCCN 2018052788| ISBN 9781788923262 (hbk : alk. paper) | ISBN 9781788923255 (pbk : alk. paper) | ISBN 9781788923293 (kindle)
Subjects: LCSH: Bilingualism in children—Parent participation. | Education—Parent participation. | Home and school. | Parent-teacher relationships.
Classification: LCC P115.2 .C63 2019 | DDC 371.19/2—dc23 LC record available at https://lccn.loc.gov/2018052788

British Library Cataloguing in Publication Data
A catalogue entry for this book is available from the British Library.

ISBN-13: 978-1-78892-326-2 (hbk)
ISBN-13: 978-1-78892-325-5 (pbk)

Multilingual Matters
UK: St Nicholas House, 31–34 High Street, Bristol BS1 2AW, UK.
USA: NBN, Blue Ridge Summit, PA, USA.

Website: www.multilingual-matters.com
Twitter: Multi_Ling_Mat
Facebook: https://www.facebook.com/multilingualmatters
Blog: www.channelviewpublications.wordpress.com

The policy of Multilingual Matters/Channel View Publications is to use papers that are natural, renewable and recyclable products, made from wood grown in sustainable forests. In the manufacturing process of our books, and to further support our policy, preference is given to printers that have FSC and PEFC Chain of Custody certification. The FSC and/or PEFC logos will appear on those books where full certification has been granted to the printer concerned.

Typeset by Nova Techset Private Limited, Bengaluru and Chennai, India.
Printed and bound in the UK by Short Run Press Ltd.
Printed and bound in the US by Thomson-Shore, Inc.

This book is dedicated to multilingual students, families and educators who live in diverse and rural settings, and who are frequently overlooked across the landscape of education. It is my sincere hope that the ideas set forth in this book pave new pathways to bring diverse people together for the betterment of our rural communities.

Contents

Tables and Figures

Acknowledgments

Family is at the heart of this book. I was a single mother of two bright and energetic children, whose education I placed as a priority in our home. My grandparents, who were first generation US immigrants and only completed school to 8th grade, were a cornerstone of my own life and upbringing. My mother herself was single for many of my formative years. I recall school events such as awards ceremonies and gym meets that required that I ask for three tickets for my mother and both grandparents to attend, not the typical two – one for each parent – that most children needed. I 'had' very little growing up in terms of financial resources, but I lacked for nothing because of my family.

In 2014, I lost my first child and only son, Thomas, to a tragic and sudden accident. He had truly a profound influence on my life and work. He had been studying biology because he wanted to work with underserved populations in healthcare. For years, both my son and daughter worked alongside me in fringe and remote rural communities in Florida. We volunteered at migrant fairs, at churches where I taught English and supported (bi)literacy development of children, advocated and interpreted in parent–teacher meetings, assisted rural families working on blueberry farms, and shuffled rural, multilingual children to dental clinics and to eye doctor appointments. For many years, I ran a mobile bilingual book project, *Libros de Familia*, where we distributed books to rural families and read together in their homes (Coady & Moore, 2010). Looking back over those years, the time I spent engaged in this work with my own family enriched our lives. We learned from the people we worked with, and we learned about each other along the way. This book is for all those named and unnamed rural multilingual families whose lives and stories are reflected in the pages of this book.

I wish to give a heartfelt acknowledgment to Deon Heffington, Shuzhan Li, Andrew Long, Mark Preston Lopez, Nidza Marichal and Aleksandra Olszewska, my research team who provided professional support and encouragement for this work and who are keen advocates for rural multilingual families. Lianne Jepson Guerra provided design expertise and multilingual inspiration. Valerie Boughanem, ESOL Coordinator, contributed her expertise, friendship and collaboration. Drs Cindy Naranjo and Paula Golombek provided extensive support for rural families and educators through coursework for Project STELLAR. Robin Lewy and Fran Ricardo, community partners and advocates for rural families, continuously offered reminders and creative solutions surrounding diverse families' needs. My husband, Tom, ensured that I had much needed space and time to write this book. I also thank the reviewers of earlier versions of this book for insight and guidance on improving the book and to Multilingual Matters, a true ally in multilingual family engagement worldwide.

About the Author

Dr Maria Coady is the Irving and Rose Fien Endowed Professor and an Associate Professor of ESOL and Bilingual Education at the University of Florida, Gainesville. She received her Doctor of Philosophy (PhD) degree from the University of Colorado, Boulder in 2001, where she was a US Department of Education Title VII Fellow between 1997 and 2001. Dr Coady's dissertation work at the University of Colorado, Boulder, investigated bilingual education programs called *Gaelscoileanna* in the Republic of Ireland. She received her Master's degree in Education (MEd) from Boston University in 1993 and Bachelor's degree in business administration and international perspectives from the University of New Hampshire, Durham. During that time, she lived worked and studied in Buenos Aires, Argentina under the Organization of American States.

Dr Coady works closely with rural multilingual students and families, at the intersection of teacher education, bilingualism and biliteracy development, and social justice issues. In 2007, she became co-Principal Investigator of a US Department of Education National Professional Development (NPD) grant, Project DELTA, that investigated the relationship between preservice teacher education and the academic learning of English language students. In 2016, she was awarded a second five-year NPD grant as Principal Investigator, which examines the rural context of education, prepares teacher-leaders for English language students and builds rural family engagement (Project STELLAR, *Supporting Teachers of English Language Learners Across Rural Settings*). Her publications include the book *Why TESOL* (5th edn), with Dr Eileen N. Whelan Ariza (Kendall Hunt Publisher). Her work also includes publications in the first *TESOL Encyclopaedia of English Language Teaching* and the journals *TESOL Quarterly*; the *Bilingual Research Journal*; *TESOL Journal*; *Language Policy*; *MEXTESOL*; and the *Journal of Language, Culture, and Communication*. Dr Coady's personal life is dedicated to working with rural multilingual populations in the memory of her son Thomas (1992–2014).

Introduction: Engaging Rural Multilingual Families: Theories and Practices

In 2010, Linda Darling-Hammond, a leading scholar of teacher education, wrote in her book *The Flat World and Education: How America's Commitment to Equity will Determine Our Future* that America's future would decidedly be determined by the quality and competency of its teachers and America's commitment to equitable education for all students. She noted that 'effective schools' are organized for both student *and* teacher learning, and those schools also ensure that teachers have time for collaboration, are able to plan together, develop curriculum and assessments, and support peer or joint examination of student work. Schools, she argued, must also address the specific challenges of local communities, families and students, including social and health care services and parent learning. Darling-Hammond believed then, and continues to acknowledge today, that the 'opportunity gap' that characterizes the quality of education between low income communities and wealthy communities in the USA must be addressed before the student achievement gap can ever be closed (Darling-Hammond, 2010: 327). What progress has been made in the ensuing decade?

This issue – high quality and equitable education for all students – is more pressing today than ever before. As a teacher educator for more than 20 years, I affirm Darling-Hammond's call to action for schools to respond to local community, family and student needs while simultaneously ensuring that there is a systemic response to student learning. Education is a complex endeavor and communities vary tremendously in terms of their needs, demographics and local cultures. Teachers, administrators, school counselors and support staff in schools have important roles to play in the education of all students, but particularly for multilingual or English learner students. It is no secret that teachers are a pivotal component in the complex process of student learning. In fact, research has shown that high quality teacher education has a positive association with student learning outcomes for children in the process of learning English as an additional language (Coady *et al.*, 2016). However, teachers and educators are not magicians and many additional factors influence student learning outcomes. Home–school relationships are one piece – often overlooked – in the complex puzzle of educational equity and student success.

Equity in Education: Inputs and Outcomes

This book underscores the essential connection that educators must make between homes and schools, not only in terms of weekly communications and school announcements, which are frequently the mainstay of 'parent communication' and dated, static and 'fossilized' practices, but also in the social, emotional and educational well-being of multilingual children living in rural settings. As educators, we cannot reverse the growing gap of academic achievement and student learning between traditional, mainstream students and students who are minoritized (Sensoy & DiAngelo, 2017), unless and until we address issues of equity and justice. Further, any relationship between schools and families who are considered 'outside the mainstream' or who represent diverse backgrounds, are subjugated to assumptions, viewpoints and social pressures that frequently fail to reflect the realities of students' lives (Hutchins *et al.*, 2012). In other words, there are vast differences between schools' and homes' orientations and beliefs towards education, particularly for multilingual families. In my work, rather than seeing educators and families come together to support student well-being and learning to challenge the social inequities that families face, the opposite seems to have occurred: families from culturally and linguistically diverse backgrounds and mainstream schools seem distant and outside of the education process now more than ever.

There are many reasons for this gap. Part of the disconnect seems to be 21st century over-emphases on testing and assessments that continue to prioritize mainstream ways of knowing and monolingual language and literacy practices at all levels: locally, nationally and internationally. While the use of standardized testing allows for international cross comparisons of student achievement (Phillips & Schweisfurth, 2014), these data focus on educational *outcomes* for students without acknowledging that the starting points or *inputs* for many children from diverse backgrounds are grossly inequitable. As the input gap continues to widen, so does the outcome. In addition, the learning practices that take place in many countries and schools emphasize monolingual, one language outcomes that underscore a single, monocultural view of the world (Makalela, 2015). This contradicts the complex, dynamic and multilingual spaces in which human interactions and behavior occur in the world today.

Equal versus equitable

In this book, I rely heavily on the distinction between equal and equitable in the context of education. *Equal refers to two or more things that are the same or given the same treatment; equitable refers to two or more things that are given the appropriate treatment or what may be optimal for growth and learning.* Educators in the current standards and standardized assessment climate sometimes mistake providing every student the same treatment (such as the same test or same instructional practices) as being 'fair', rather than ensuring that a student assessment is based on student mastery of skills using individual growth scales, portfolio assessments or differentiated materials such as a bilingual graphic organizer (Gee, 2003). Specific to multilingual students, educational practices need to respond to and reflect the multiple language systems that students can access cognitively and that represent their multilingual ways of knowing and being in the world. Research today in this area continues to examine how multilingual students use their entire linguistic repertoires when 'languaging' (García, 2009: 23). Well-planned and differentiated instruction for multilingual children whereby they are able to access and expand their use of languages is an equitable educational strategy.

Standardization of education is problematic for students and families from different language backgrounds when their language is not a resource for learning in school (García, 2016; Ruiz, 1984), a practice that sadly persists in schools worldwide. For example, a teacher who teaches 5th grade science must assess their students using a standards-driven test. They want to assess their students to make sure that they have mastered the scientific concepts or standards of the lesson and they think that giving all students the same test is the fairest way to do so. However, some of her students know the concepts using a different language or need to make sense of the terminology, sentence structure, context and meaning using different languages (Li & Luo, 2017). The students can reason, demonstrate and describe the scientific process they learned in class, and they could perform well on the test if it were given in languages in which they could best communicate their knowledge. However, students might be unable to describe the results of an experiment in great detail because they do not have access to the scientific language associated with the concepts on an English-only test. Has the teacher assessed the students' learning of scientific concepts? Has she assessed their English language ability? Or has she assessed both? Is giving the same science test 'fair' to all of her students?

Despite research that repeatedly confirms the academic and social benefits of using students' first language in learning (Collier & Thomas, 2017; MacSwan *et al.*, 2017), educational policies and teacher practices continue to operate from a position of 'time on task' (MacSwan *et al.*, 2017), in which the more time multilingual students spend in the majority language (such as English) will yield higher academic outcomes for students. Data from studies conducted by many educational scholars simply reject that theory. Unfortunately for multilingual students and families, educational policies continue to be passed based on invalid assumptions about second language learning. For instance, in Florida, the state has used its English-only political status to deny multilingual students access to first language assessments that would more accurately demonstrate their learning and achievement (Mitchell, 2018).

In addition, today's educational practices that are driven solely by standards and student learning outcomes, though useful as comparative data, can be counter-productive to educational equity. It is increasingly difficult to interrogate the social grand narratives and ideologies in our education systems that fail to include multilingual children and families, their knowledge and use of languages, and their diverse backgrounds. Neoliberal views, where education is considered a commodity in a market economy in which parents are shoppers and customers, has pervaded urban and rural schools alike. Reynolds (2017: xxi), who writes about rural education, describes how the consequences of 'neoliberal money obsessed ideology... are horrific', particularly for rural schools. Yet the tensions that educators face as they navigate educational policies against the lived realities of their students is real on a daily basis. Educators are frustrated, confused, silenced and feel defeated. What is refreshing about rural schools and the educators who work in them is that many stay the course, are committed to their communities and work to improve student learning.

Recently, I was meeting a rural principal at a school in Florida. We were discussing the prior few years at the school and the urgent issue of teacher retention in her rural elementary school, More than 50% of her fourth grade teachers were substitutes that year (2017–18). Over the prior three years, she lost five teachers alone who were within their first three years of entering the teaching profession. She herself had served in education for almost 40 years. She was looking forward to retirement and working on her family farm where she raised cattle, and she was considering working with dairy cows so that she could make butter with an antique butter churn that had been in her mother's family for generations.

The principal's commitment to the rural community in which she lives lit up her face. She recognized the challenges facing rural educators: poverty, hunger, and extremely limited resources, access to healthcare and technology, and distance to necessary social services. But over the years she had identified some viable opportunities: the schools as central, community spaces; teacher and student mentorships; and some home–school connections. Ultimately, she felt that without personal relationships between teachers and caregivers, and schools and homes, quality education was not possible for rural students. Her response to teachers who bemoaned being unable to communicate or reach rural parents was, 'be ready at 2:45 and we'll drive out to the home together.'

Ultimately, what do we know about engaging multilingual families who live and work in rural settings? What do teachers need to know? And how can we all work toward developing what Bryk and Schneider (2002) refer to as 'relational trust' with rural, multilingual families?

This book aims to illuminate several key points that have not been well developed or articulated in prior work on rural multilingual families and the schools that multilingual children attend. I see the work of rural education for multilingual families in its early stages, though I recognize that there have been important inroads made in recent years into understanding diversity in rural settings. There is, however, much left for us to know and do. Educators working in rural schools need an understanding of who families are, what they know, and how they function, survive and thrive in diverse and varied rural settings. As described throughout this book, multilingual families speak, use, read, write and understand multiple languages. Their language and knowledge of different semiotic systems reflect their identities (ontology) and the way that they come to know and participate in the world (epistemology).

The problem with traditional models of family engagement is that they frequently default to a list of strategies that cannot possibly respond to the varied sociohistorical backgrounds of families, the political influences that affect families and children's lives or that are differentiated to respond to their needs. Also problematic is that those strategies overlook educators' views, beliefs, experiences and expectations about family engagement.

Throughout this book I note that multiple systems interact and influence a child's school experiences. Families who are immigrant, migrant, refugee or permanently settled in rural settings function in ways that may differ from teacher expectations and what schools iterate and enact as family engagement. Teacher views of what effective family engagement is have remained static over time. However, there is no monolithic demographic that encompasses all multilingual families in rural settings and educational practices must be re-align and continually renegotiated with rural multilingual families. Hence, a first step for educators is reflection and learning about multilingual families and how they function, survive and thrive in different rural communities.

The second point follows the first. Any set of strategies, even those identified as most 'effective' for family engagement, cannot accurately meet the needs of all families. Countless frameworks call for home-language communication strategies for families that default into a list of items. For example, few would deny that communicating in a language used in a child's home is an effective way to share information with families. However, even in today's multilingual world, it remains challenging for educators to use home languages to convey important school material and events (Coady et al., 2008). Despite these fossilized practices, scholars note the importance of the diversity in family engagement and the conditions under which home–school partnerships are built (Semke & Sheridan, 2012). Yet more research is warranted in this area, and much more support must be levied across rural setting in general and with multilingual families in particular, in order to meet that goal.

For educators to truly engage rural multilingual families, their work must be built upon trust, care, understanding and human relationships. In their study of one home–school intervention program, Teachers and Parents as Partners (TAPP), Sheridan *et al.* (2014: 271) found that 'partnerships between families and schools are couched in relationships, developed and refined through intentional interactions over time'. Similarly, the critical pedagogue Michael Apple (2016) implores us to examine the 'relational' aspect of education, noting how social structures perpetuate inequities and difference across groups. Apple (2016, n.p.) argues that education 'can only be understood by its connections to relations of dominance and subordination in the larger society.' These relations seem more pressing in rural settings where families and schools have been absent from conversations regarding educational programs for English learner and multilingual families.

Over time, my work in rural communities with multilingual families has evolved from learning *about* families to learning *with* families and learning *from* families. I recall a recent family engagement meeting where a father, Esteban, entered the double glass doors of the school library. I knew Esteban from 10 years prior, when he was a young man in a rural community adult English as a second language program that I ran in a local library. We immediately recognized each other. Ten years later, he entered the school media center with his three children and wife. We could not recall exactly the last time we had seen each other, but we were both still invested in rural education, shifting our perspectives from learner to parent, and from teacher to director. The importance of time and commitment to families in rural communities is crucial. Over time, families see us as helpful partners in the education and well-being of their children. They trust us.

Third, education would benefit from a framework that conceptualizes multilingual family engagement situated in its sociohistorical and political context and the realities of the lived experiences of children and families. This is essential in order for educators to not only build relationships and relational trust with families, but to advocate for families and transform educational policies and practices that continue to marginalize and disempower them. Rural schools in particular can be are sites of resistance and that challenge social inequities (John & Ford, 2017). Moreover, rural schools are pivotal and are often the only physical space in rural communities where families, children and educators can come together and voice concerns, identify solutions and support each other.

In 2017 in our rural setting in north Florida, we experienced a series of hurricanes that swept through the area. Families, many of who were poor and lived in unsafe housing, were forced to evacuate their homes and relocate to schools during the severe weather. Others, however, remained in their homes to bear the brunt of the deadly storms. Rural teachers were anxious to return to school before the storms had cleared, because they understood that every day that children were home was a day that the children and families might not eat. Rural school sites frequently take on the role of community centers, address food security, are emergency home shelters, and even offer a venue for entertainment and movie nights.

In this book, I describe five principles that help to differentiate rural multilingual family engagement across two areas: reflection and action. The five principles include listening to and learning about multilingual families' cultures, languages and literacy practices; reflecting on families' strengths and gaining input from community members; communicating and building relational trust with families in ways that align home cultures and languages to schools; using knowledge of families to support students' learning; and advocating for equity and change in and outside of school.

Notably, the first two of these principles involve self-awareness, reflection and educators' building or extending their own knowledge base. How teachers understand, for example, the different backgrounds and migration patterns between Venezuelan, Puerto Rican or Guatemalan students in the USA is crucial in their actions towards fostering family engagement. No longer can educators remain unaware or ignorant of these political grand narratives, international human migration trends and economic policies that affect rural communities (Reynolds, 2017). Like humans ourselves, these are interconnected trends and issues, and at the micro-level they affect the education of the child.

These realities shape and form future actions of advocacy and change for rural schools, rural educators and multilingual families. Questions about what languages and literacies are taught and for what purposes should be at the forefront of all educators' practices and conversations when working with multilingual children. Moreover, educational practices that support the languages and literacy development such as translanguaging reflect teachers' and school-based ideologies regarding the value and use of multiple languages in schools. I see those conversations, reflections, decisions and instructional practices as a step forward in a post-colonial, post-structural world, where languages, like groups of people, are siloed and separated. This is the intersection of the school, teacher practices and educational policies.

Goals of this Book

This book is about engaging rural multilingual families and children in relationships that support families and their children's learning. While I review extensive research on family engagement, this is not uniquely a research-focused book. Rather, this book aims to review research from the field and connect readers with resources that teachers, practitioners and teacher-educators can use and adapt with multilingual families in rural settings. In my work as a scholar and teacher educator, I consider the step of connecting research to practice as necessary and *translational*. Translational research is analogous to the 'bench to bedside' movement in the field of medicine. It takes research findings and provides examples of their application to schools and classrooms. The materials provided in this book, located in Chapters 3–5, are starting points for educator discussions and adaptations and should not be misconstrued as one-size-fits-all hand-outs, because every school is varied and richly complex. By complex I am referring to the multiple languages, cultures, resources, identities and ways of knowing that can be found inside a school. I recognize that there is no shortcut to engaging rural multilingual families and no single approach to the education of any child.

This book is a response to the large number of scripted programs and lists of educational 'best practices' for family engagement that frequently have little to do with the realities of the multilingual families and children living in our rural communities in the USA, my primary context, and outside of the USA, where I have worked in teacher education and family engagement for many years. This book does not intend to provide a set of definitive practices that 'work' for families or marginalized groups. I echo the work of Lopez (2001: 420), who aptly notes, 'such a move would only reify the normality of involvement while perpetuating the belief that these parents are not involved in the educational lives of their children'. Nothing could be further from the truth. My goal is to reframe our view of multi-lingual families, expand upon the existing research by introducing a model of differentiated family engagement for rural multilingual families, and provide educators with opportunities to use activities and materials that derive from theory and research. These resources are meant to be adapted, interrogated, enhanced, discarded and/or improved in ways that reflect local classrooms, schools and community contexts.

Organization and Audience

This book is organized in eight chapters. Each chapter begins with chapter highlights and ends with discussion questions, application and activities to connect the information to local settings. The book begins with an overview of some of the current complexities in education, noted above, with an emphasis on diversity within and across multilingual communities in rural settings. In the first chapter, I review today's 21st century global environment, the changing nature of education, and the multilingual characteristics of families and students. Next, I define and narrow in on family engagement for families who use and speak languages in the home that differ from those used in school (Coady & Yilmaz, 2017). Finally, I describe the unique needs of multilingual families in rural spaces, where transportation, food security, medical care, social services, technology and social networks are stretched and often beyond the reach of many families today.

Chapter 2 includes a review of literature related to multilingual family engagement by framing the issue from a 'strengths-based approach'. By strengths, I aim to reframe the deficit paradigm of nontraditional families who reside in rural settings and to identify and acknowledge the contributions that they make. I review research on family engagement, then frame this book conceptually using a Freirean lens of equity and linguistically responsive pedagogy. This chapter concludes with the concept of relational trust and care, which I argue are essential to building relationships with families.

Chapter 3 continues the discussion on engagement by reviewing and extending several common models of family engagement by educators and scholars in the field. Some of the models focus on multilingual families in particular (such as Arias & Morillo-Campbell (2008) and the WIDA A, B, Cs of parent engagement), while others do not (Henderson & Mapp, 2002, and Epstein, 2011). Importantly, although those frameworks represent largely Western ideologies and views of families, they are a departure point for conceptualizing and expanding this important work. Chapter 3 argues for differentiated family engagement as a way for educators to center their work with families. I introduce a model for educators that includes five essential features. Although neither sequential nor meant to be directive, these features of family engagement include: educators learning about multilingual families' languages, cultures, literacy practices and needs; educators reflecting upon their community context and seeking input from leaders and informants. Educators then use their knowledge of families and their local community to invite, engage and interact with families on an ongoing basis. They connect their knowledge of families and their sociohistorical and political context to make instructional decisions in classrooms and the school that reveal and reflect the realities of their multilingual students' lives. Finally, educators advocate for families in and outside of school with a critical eye toward social change that affirms families' languages and cultures.

Chapters 4 and 5 provide two sides to multilingual family engagement. These are theoretically-informed and based on years of research with rural multilingual families. The practical materials are for use, adaptation and expansion. Chapter 4 focuses on educators learning about the needs of rural, multilingual families and children, while Chapter 5 consists of actions that educators can take. Chapter 6 describes the grand narratives of immigration, poverty and rurality that Latino families and children face in the current sociopolitical context of the USA. This chapter uses an ecological social systems model by Bronfenbrenner (1994) to aid in understanding how grand narratives affect children and families. Chapter 7 is a co-authored chapter by a family-community advocacy group, the Rural Women's Health Project (rwhp.org), which has engaged in international work with rural multilingual families for nearly 25 years. The authors offer insights into schools and rural multilingual families from a community agency perspective, a lens frequently missing from books for educators. Finally, Chapter 8 provides new directions for 21st century multilingual family engagement.

This book is a research-driven and theoretically-informed volume intended for teachers, educators and teacher-educators who work in rural settings with linguistically diverse, multilingual families and children. It is intended to connect those theories to educational practices. Parts of this book, including many of the activities, could be applied to preservice teachers as they begin their careers and will likely encounter multilingual students during their tenure as educators. The challenge before us is to dispel myths about multilingual families as one monolithic group. Educators working in rural settings will likely connect with the need to better understand the context of rurality, the social processes that occur in those settings, and its intersection with cultural and linguistic diversity. While rural schools face challenges related to poverty, teacher retention and education for diverse learners, and resources, they are sites of learning, spaces for community and venues of opportunity to reconceptualize and build relationships with multilingual families.

References

Apple, M.W. (2016) Power, policy, and the realities of curriculum and teaching. Paper presented at Ljubljana Center for Educational Policy Studies. Univerza V. Ljubljani Pedagoska fakulteta. See https://youtu.be/YcPv0Pk7Uqs

Arias, M.B. and Morillo-Campbell, M. (2008) Promoting ELL parental involvement: Challenges in contested times. Boulder, CO: Education Policy Research Unit. ERIC document ED506652. Retrieved from https://eric.ed.gov/?id=ED506652

Bronfenbrenner, U. (1994) Ecological models of human development. *International Encyclopedia of Education*, 3 (2), 1643–1647. Oxford, UK: Elsevier Sciences.

Bryk, A.S. and Schneider, B. (2002) *Trust in Schools: A Score Resource for Improvement.* New York: Russell Sage Foundation.

Coady, M.R. and Yilmaz, T. (2017) Preparing teachers of ELs: Home-school partnerships. *TESOL Encyclopedia of English Language Teaching*. Hoboken, NJ: Wiley.

Coady, M., Cruz-Davis, J. and Flores, C. (2008) *Personalmente*: Home-school communication practices with (im)migrant families in north Florida. Special Topics Issue, *Bilingual Research Journal* 31 251–270. See https://www.tandfonline.com/doi/full/10.1080/15235880802640714

Coady, M., Harper, C. and de Jong, E. (2016) Aiming for equity: Preparing mainstream teachers for inclusion or inclusive classrooms? *TESOL Quarterly* 50 (2), 340–368. DOI: 10.1002/tesq.223

Collier, V. P. and Thomas, W.P. (2017) Validating the power of bilingual schooling: Thirty-two years of large-scale longitudinal research. *Annual Review of Applied Linguistics* 37, 203–217.

Darling-Hammond, L. (2010) *The Flat World and Education: How America's Commitment to Equity will Determine Our Future*. New York: Teachers College Press.

Epstein, J. L. (2011) School, *Family, and Community Partnerships: Preparing Educators and Improving Schools* (2nd edn). Philadelphia, PA: Westview Press.

García, O. (2009) *Bilingual Education in the 21st Century: A Global Perspective*. Malden, MA: John Wiley.

García, O. (2016) *Translanguaging with Multilingual Students: Learning from Classroom Moments*. New York: Routledge.

Gee, J. (2003) Opportunity to learn: a language based perspective on assessment. *Assessment in Education* 10 (1), 27–46.

Henderson, A.T. and Mapp, K.L. (2002) *A New Wave of Evidence: The Impact of School, Family and Community Connections on Student Achievement*. Austin, TX: Southwest Educational Development Laboratory. Retrieved from www.sedl.org/connections/resources/evidence.pdf

Hutchins, D.J., Greenfeld, M.D., Epstein, J.L., Sanders, M.G. and Galindo, C. (2012) *Multicultural Partnerships: Involve All Families*. Larchmont, NY: Eye on Education.

John, K.D. and Ford, D.R. (2017) The rural is nowhere: Bringing Indigeneity and urbanism into educational research. In W.M. Reynolds (ed). *Forgotten Places: Critical Studies in Rural Education* (pp. 3–14). New York: Peter Lang.

Kress, G. (2009) *Multimodality: A Social Semiotic Approach to Contemporary Communication*. New York: Routledge.

Li, S. and Luo, W. (2017) Creating a translanguaging space for high school emergent bilinguals. *CATESOL Journal* 29 (2), 139–162.

Lopez, G. (2001) The value of hard work: Lessons on parent involvement from an (im)migrant household. *Harvard Educational Review* 71 (3), 416–438.

MacSwan, J., Thompson, M.S., Rolsad, K., McAlister, K. and Lobo, G. (2017) Three theories of the effects of language education programs: An empirical evaluation of bilingual and English-only policies. *Annual Review of Applied Linguistics* 37, 218–240. Retrieved from https://doi.org/10.1017/S0267190517000137

Makalela, L. (2015) Bilingualism in South Africa: Reconnecting with *Ubuntu* translanguaging. In O. García and A. Lin (eds) *Encyclopedia of Bilingualism and Bilingual Education* (pp. 297–309). New York: Springer.

Mitchell, C. (2018) DeVos's Approval of Florida's ESSA Plan. *Education Week*. See http://blogs.edweek.org/edweek/learning-the-language/2018/09/devos_approves_floridas_essa_plan_english_learners.html

Phillips, D. and Schweisfurth, M. (2014) *Comparative and International Education* (2nd edn). New York: Bloomsbury.

Reynolds, W. (2017) *Forgotten Places: Critical Studies in Rural Education*. New York: Peter Lang.

Ruiz, R. (1984) Orientations in language planning. *NABE Journal* 8 (2), 15–34.

Semke, C.A. and Sheridan, S.M. (2012) Family-school connections in rural educational settings: A systematic review of the empirical literature. *School Community Journal* 22 (1), 21–48.

Sensoy, Ö. and DiAngelo, R.J. (2017) *Is Everyone Really Equal?: An Introduction to Key Concepts in Social Justice Education* (2nd edn). New York: Teachers College Press.

Sheridan, S.M., Kunz, G.M., Holmes, S. and Witte, A. (2017) Family-school partnerships in rural communities: Benefits, exemplars and future research. In G.C. Nugent, G.M. Kunz, S.M. Sheridan, T.A. Glover and L.L. Knoche (eds) *Rural Education Research in the United States: State of the Science and Emerging Directions* (pp. 269–290). Switzerland: Springer International.

1 Rural Multilingual Family Engagement in the 21st Century

Highlights

- Growth and diversity in multilingual communities.
- Key terminology multilingual, immigrant, migrant, migration networks, *familismo*.
- Rurality as false binary.
- Parent and family engagement across diverse communities.
- Challenges and opportunities for rural educators and multilingual families.
- Activities for further learning.

Introduction

This chapter examines rurality and multilingualism for family engagement. The sections elaborate upon terminology that will be used throughout the book. Essentially, how we refer to people, such as multilinguals, and places, such as rural, is arguably a difficult task, because the process of labeling positions people and places in categories and boxes that fail to reflect diversity within categories and across spaces. Thus, the terminology here aims to complicate those categories and to illuminate how prior work on parent involvement, for example, has established narrow views of multilingual families, particularly in rural settings.

Growth and Diversity in Multilingual Communities

What are multilingual communities in the context of education? Multilingual communities are spaces where two or more languages are used on a regular basis. Multilingual communities can also be conceptualized as physical or geographic areas that are frequently located in urban, rural, suburban, and semi-rural settings in addition to virtual spaces, where multiple languages are used as mediums for communication, such as online messaging and gaming.

Throughout this book, I refer to English learner (EL) students, bilingual students or emerging bilingual (EB) students broadly as *multilingual students*. I use the term multilingual as a purposeful departure from the term 'bi' lingual, which limits conversations about language to two (bi-) languages, when in fact multiple language varieties – including what are referred to as dialects – are used increasingly worldwide. In addition, bilingual underscores the separation of languages and does not fully capture the varied language systems that are often overlooked in rural settings where the number of multilinguals might be small relative to urban settings. In addition to language, this book acknowledges how semiotic systems contribute to linguistic repertoires. Semiotic systems are also used and accessed in rural communities by multilinguals. Examples of semiotic systems involve interacting on the worldwide web via the internet, text features, gestures, signs and symbols (Coady & Ariza, 2010; Kress, 2009; Li & Luo, 2017; Li et al., 2014).

Multilingualism across 21st century global environments is so pervasive, it is more difficult to identify communities that are uniquely *mono*lingual, as opposed to communities that are *multi*lingual. Here, again, I acknowledge the tension between using terminology that sets up a binary (mono versus multilingual) and the need to understand language uses and purposes. Today, multilinguals outnumber monolinguals worldwide and in Europe more than 50% of people claim to speak more than one language (European Commission, 2012). Recent data indicate that, although Americans lag behind their European counterparts in terms of multiple language proficiency and use, more than 21% of Americans claim to use more than one language in the household (American Community Survey, 2014).

Consider the country of South Africa, which has about 55 million people. Following the official end of apartheid in 1991, South Africa declared 11 languages as official, including isiZulu, Afrikaans, English, isiXhosa, Sepedi, Setswana, Sesotho, Xitsonga, SiSwati, Tshivenda and isiNdebele. In most places in South Africa, people speak multiple languages and transition smoothly between those languages for communicative purposes (Makalela, 2015). This phenomenon can be observed on television, heard on the radio and read in social media outlets, as well as in stores, restaurants and school spaces. The concept of strategically communicating across multiple languages for communication is referred to in education as *translanguaging*. Translanguaging occurs naturally among multilinguals in South Africa; for example, where students speak multiple languages. Translanguaging as an educational practice exists in a variety of school settings, from English-dominant content area classrooms and bilingual education programs in the USA (García, 2016; Li & Luo, 2017) to mother tongue education programs in the Philippines (Lopez & Coady,

2018) and South Africa (Makalela, 2016). We will return to the topic of multiple language use in school settings later on in this book in the context of working with rural multilingual families.

It is easy to see how multiple languages and semiotic systems can be used in virtual spaces. For example, youth today engage in online gaming as one activity and use multiple languages in virtual international spaces such as *World of Warcraft* (Li *et al.*, 2014). In addition, websites from nonprofit organizations to nongovernmental organizations (NGOs) to multinational institutions and even urban schools offer websites in multiple languages as a way to convey information to broader, multilingual audiences.

Human migration in the 21st century

In the context of international human migration, when individuals or groups of people move into new settings, there is an increase in language contact and the use of multiple languages. Multiple language use is a response to and result of global human migration patterns where individuals and groups emigrate (leave) or immigrate (enter). In a partner school in South Africa, I examined the writing practices of multilingual children (Coady *et al.*, 2018). The children were writing in English and isiZulu, because those two languages were used for literacy purposes in school. I interviewed children after they wrote and was surprised to learn that several of the children had emigrated from Congo and spoke French, in addition to the languages used in school and the community. When I asked children to describe their 'first' language, they looked perplexed. Within their multilingual community, English and isiZulu were used in school and for literacy purposes, but many spoke and used isiXhosa and Sepedi. Students could not identify a first language because conceptually they did not have just one. Those students capture the realities of multilinguals who communicate across languages for specific purposes. I like to think of languaging among multilinguals as 'uber languaging', like the ubiquitous Uber car taxi system where drivers come from, traverse and travel to many places.

The Migration Policy Institute in the USA tracks the net number of migrants who move around the world by country, from 1950 through 2015 (Migration Policy Institute, 2015). Not surprisingly, the USA leads all countries in the world in net in-migration, with more than 5 million immigrants relocating to the USA between the years 2010 and 2015 (Figure 1.1). Syria and India lead the world in net emigration, with war-torn Syrian refugees experiencing high out-migration. As of 2014, the total number of international migrants reached 244 million, or over 3% of the world's population (Migration Policy Institute, 2017). Often, migrants move to countries where the language of schooling differs from the language used in the home. The effects of human migration globally are definitely

Net Number of Migrants by Country, 1950-2015 (by Five-Year Intervals)

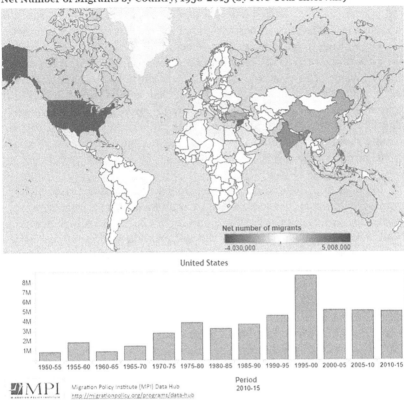

Figure 1.1 Net number of immigrants
Source: Migration Policy Institute (MPI)

experienced locally when children who speak languages other than the dominant school language enter school and when educators and families communicate. In today's complex human migration context and the effects of migration on schooling, educators face the essential tasks of building from students' home and multiple languages to support their learning.

One of the greatest assets of multilingual families is the linguistic diversity and the global perspectives that they bring to schools and communities, such as their diversity in thought, cultural practices and life experiences. Yet multilinguals are frequently subjected to educational policies and practices that de-value or that fail to acknowledge their linguistic knowledge (Fernández & López, 2017; López, 2001) and cultural parenting styles (Goodall & Vorhaus, 2010; Hutchins *et al.*, 2012).

Take, for example, the story of Tania Luna (Luna, 2012). Tania was an immigrant asylum seeker to the USA after the devastating nuclear plant accident that took place on April 26, 1986 in Chernobyl, Ukraine. Tania and her family experienced physical and emotional trauma as a result of the accident, including sicknesses and her sister's loss of hair. After several years of waiting to relocate, Tania and her family were granted permission to immigrate to the USA. However, her new life in the USA was not a simple matter of relocation. Tania and her family faced linguistic differences and culture shock, and they struggled to survive while living in extreme poor conditions. Tania and her family managed to integrate into schools and a new community over time. When they returned to their humble start, only then did they realize the magnitude of what they had experienced. Tania shares her heartfelt story, *How a penny made me feel like a millionaire*, on a TED talk.

Tania is not alone. The International Rescue Committee (IRC), a global NGO, notes that there are more than 65 million displaced persons worldwide (International Rescue Committee , 2017). This includes about 40 million people who are displaced *within* their own home countries. Some are women and children affected by conflict and natural disasters, others are families who seek safety from war, and still others are displaced youth and adults seeking economic opportunities to support basic survival (food, shelter, healthcare). Many refugees wait years, if not decades, for the legal right to relocate (emigrate) to other countries. The current president of the IRC, David Miliband, implores us that 'the great danger [this century] is that we are consumed by our divisions, and there is no better test of that than how we treat refugees... it is a test of our humanity' (Miliband, 2017). Human migration is a political, social and economic issue, and educators worldwide must be aware of the international issues that affect their students and families who may be present in their very own classrooms.

Asylum seekers are people who seek refuge under the 1951 Refugee Convention on the Status of Refugees. People seek asylum when they believe that they will face imminent persecution based on race, religion, political belief, nationality or membership in a particular social group in their country of origin, such as sexual orientation. Asylum seekers and refugees are immigrants when they relocate to a new country. They often have no choice but to leave behind their loved-ones, friends, customs, cultural practices and often languages. This is a harsh experience that is not easily navigated. The effects of migration are especially difficult on children who have no say in the decision to migrate or the maturity to understand why families undertake such a traumatic event (Datta, 2004).

Terminology in the context of the USA

The term migrant, defined above by the Migration Policy Institute, differs from the term 'migrant' in the context of some countries such as the USA. Consider the terms immigrant, emigrant and migrant. The word root 'migrant' stems from the Latin *migrare*, which means *to remove, depart, move from one place to another*. In the US context, migrants are people who work in seasonal agriculture, fishing or dairy industries and who move frequently following harvests, temporal labor demands and industries. Vocke (2007: 3) refers to migrant workers as 'invisible people' based on their status as one of the most marginalized and undereducated populations in the USA. Despite documentary films such as *Harvest of Shame*, which was broadcast in 1960 and re-released 50 years later (CBS, 2010), Americans know little about the struggles and contributions of migrant workers to the US economy. Because of the farm work that migrants do in harvest and crop industries, they often reside in rural settings.

Many migrant workers today in the USA are immigrants. Children of migrant farmworkers in the USA experience the effects of seasonal labor work such as poverty, disparities among different US states' curriculums and graduation requirements, and language and cultural differences (Salinas & Fránquiz, 2004). In order to qualify for specialized services in schools, the migrant farmworking parents must move or cross school district lines in pursuit of more work (US Department of Education, 2018). Children of migrant workers in the USA receive supplemental educational support to assist them while they are learning in school settings. Some children receive additional support with a migrant education tutor. In contrast to this narrow definition, a common international term for migrant refers to human movement and relocation.

A problem with labeling groups of people is that there is a wealth of diversity within the broad categories of 'immigrant', 'migrant' or 'multilingual'. Some immigrants, for example, are simultaneously migrant farmworkers in the US context, while other immigrants move to the USA as refugees who have faced extensive persecution and discrimination in their home countries. Recent refugees and crises include Syria, due to its ongoing civil war, while others, like Tania Luna from Eastern Europe, seek refuge after a domestic disaster. As Figure 1.2 displays, in 2015 the largest sending country was Mexico, which accounted for 29.3% of total immigrants to the USA. India accounts for 5.5% of immigrants and China accounts for 4.8%. However, 'other' sending countries taken as a whole accounts for the majority of immigrants at 42.3%.

An additional concept related to migration in the 21st century is the pattern of establishing migration networks, a process sometimes referred to as chain migration. Chain migration occurs when families, relatives or friends immigrate to a geographic space following someone who emigrated at an earlier date. In the geographic space, immigrants establish networks that build social, cultural, linguistic and community support for one another. The phenomenon of *migration networking* affects rural multilingual children and families, when groups of immigrants continue to arrive and schools are unprepared for the languages and cultures of immigrants.

Top Ten Largest U.S. Immigrant Groups, 2015

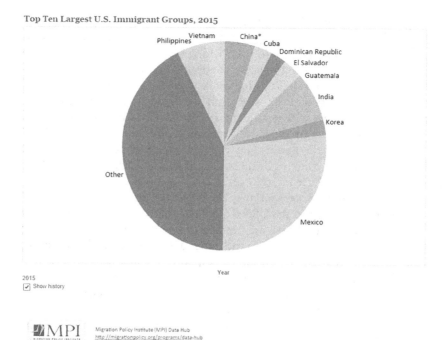

Figure 1.2 Top 10 largest US immigrant groups
Source: Migration Policy Institute (MPI)

Large-scale migration patterns continue worldwide. For example, migrants travel in search of labor and later send for their spouse, children or extended families to join them. The pattern of migration networking was great in the USA during the industrial age, when there was a need for labor in factories. For example, immigrants from a small town outside of Naples, Italy, resettled to a small enclave in Stoneham, Massachusetts, bypassing Ellis Island and making their way directly to 10 miles north of Boston where they had relatives and an established social support network. Similar patterns exist today and recent trends have captured how immigrant families settle in locales not previously settled by immigrants in prior decades. In these 'new destination settings', educators may be un- or underprepared to work with multilingual families and children (Suro & Singer, 2013).

Although many immigrants come to the USA from Latin America, and Mexico is the top sending country to the USA, not all immigrants from Latin America have similar educational experiences or backgrounds, not all speak Spanish and not all emigrate for the same reasons. In fact, within the Latino population, there are hundreds of different languages spoken and many varieties of Spanish, Portuguese, Dutch, French and indigenous languages. The languages spoken by immigrant Latinos reflect

Figure 1.3 Immigrant family
Source: M. Coady

rich histories, cultures, identities and ways of knowing, which are essential to the culture's survival and the identity development of children (Figure 1.3).

Multilingual Family Engagement

Many multilingual students have multiple languages and literacy practices, home culture, rituals and routines. Some rural communities have become settlement venues for immigrants or refugees. Some families engage in more familial child rearing practices, while others reflect a more traditional, nuclear family structure. A child's learning is affected as much by their experiences outside of school as it is inside. In short, the role that families play in a child's education, and the linguistic and cultural backgrounds of children and families are deeply connected to student learning.

The widely varied experiences of families and their personal educational histories should alert us to the fact that there is not a single set of standard practices that educators should follow in the context of family engagement. Some of the existing research and literature on family engagement identifies either the barriers to engagement (Zimmerman-Orozco, 2011) or some corresponding strategies that educators can use (Ferlazzo, 2009; Haneda & Alexander, 2015; Taniguchi & Hirakawa, 2016). However, as this book puts forth, rural multilingual family engagement must be differentiated and contextualized, and is ultimately predicated on a foundation of human relationships and trust (or 'relational trust', see Bryk & Schneider, 2002) and care.

In this book I use the term 'family' to include not only biological parents but also nonbiological parents, caregivers and extended family members who are frequently involved in children's educational experiences. Across some cultural groups, for example, caregiver responsibilities may involve grandparents, aunts, uncles, cousins or even more distant relatives who share caregiving for children. It is not uncommon, for example, for Asian grandmothers to live with their children for six months, a year, or longer after the birth of a grandchild. The family structure is one of interdependence and these different parenting practices are important for educators to recognize across different racial, ethnic and linguistic groups.

Edgell and Docka (2007) conducted a study of families and gender ideology in diverse religious communities. They looked at three different religious settings to examine gender ideologies and families: a Hispanic Catholic parish, an African American black congregation and a white liberal Protestant congregation. All three religious settings were considered liberal in both their views and definitions of family. The authors found a wide range of ideologies related to family and gender, innovation in family inclusion practices by the congregations and affirmation of nontraditional gender practices. Based on these authors' findings, the local religious communities played an important role in inclusion of nontraditional, diverse families in local settings. They also found that gender roles and families were ideologically complex.

The inclusive definition of family here contrasts with government definitions that guide educational policies and practices in schools. The US Department of Education defines parent as a *legal guardian* who lives with the child and who is legally responsible for the child's welfare. Educators must navigate the differing cultural backgrounds and parenting practices of children along with legal definitions that guide their work with students. The notion of having a legal representative or guardian who is ultimately responsible for the child does not necessarily reflect the actual caregiver practices of the home. In other words, a parent may be the legal guardian of a child but not the caregiver responsible for the child's education, meals and healthcare.

Throughout the book, I use the broader definition of family, as opposed to parent, to reflect the multiple configurations and definitions of a 'family'. Where the term 'parent' is used, it is intended to be inclusive of all caregivers who provide support for children in temporary or permanent housing arrangements, who make decisions for the welfare and social-emotional well-being of children, or caregivers who provide foster care for children and youths.

In similar vein, I use the term 'engagement' in a broad sense to include all of the home practices, expectations and experiences of caregivers that support student learning and overall well-being. Ceballo *et al.* (2014) describe parental involvement as resources parents dedicate to their children's education, namely 'parents' interactions with schools and with their children to promote academic success' (Hill & Tyson, 2009: 741). The concept of 'involvement' assumes that parents or families are responsible for and initiate actions and interactions with schools. This is a narrower view of the actual activities, supports and experiences of families in the context of a child's education. In contrast, I underscore the term 'engagement' to emphasize the effort on the part of educators to reach out, know, understand, care and advocate for students in collaboration with parents and caregivers.

Research on family engagement from the USA

The research and literature on family engagement highlights several practices that are common: *communication* and interactions that take place between families and educators (Deslandes *et al.*, 1997) and that respond to the cultural and linguistic repertoires of families; varied types of *participation* in and outside of school, ranging from more traditional school events such as parent–teacher conferences to family culture fairs to home literacy events (Coady, 2009; Miedel & Reynolds, 1999); and *assistance for* children that supports home learning, strengthens family relationships and supports child well-being (Shumow & Miller, 2001). We know now that effective family engagement also includes much broader activities such as home *conversations* about the importance and value of education. For example, among Latinos in the USA, research has found that the concept of *familismo* – maintaining close bonds with family, family obligations and maintaining familial support networks – influenced how parents or caregivers interacted with their child in school-related tasks and expectations (Niemeyer *et al.*, 2009; Sabogal *et al.*, 1987).

Jeynes's (2003) review provides additional insight into effective parental involvement. In his analysis of research related to parental involvement (that author's term), Jeynes (2003) identified some important findings regarding the factors that influenced student learning. Jeynes reviewed and analyzed 77 research studies related to parental involvement, including diverse groups of students and families. Jeynes found two main areas that appeared to significantly affect student learning. The first factor was parental (caregiver) *communication* with the child, including conversations related to school experiences, home learning and the importance of education. The second factor that affected student learning was conveying high *expectations* of the child. Some of those high expectations involved supporting the students' schoolwork and expectations for future education, such as attending college. Jeynes' work shows that parental involvement, broadly defined, has a significant and positive effect on children across different race, ethnic, social class and linguistic groups.

Similary, Henderson and Mapp (2002) analyzed 51 studies related to family involvement in US K-12 public schools. They found that family engagement had a strong positive association with student achievement.

Importantly, the kinds of family engagement that was most effective was that which built upon families' strengths, recognized class difference, cultural difference and addressed specific family needs. This research is important for all educators of EL students to note, because it demonstrates that parental engagement includes nontraditional forms of educational participation. For example, educators may believe that parents should have a physical presence in schools or classrooms in order to be involved in their child's education. In contrast, Jeynes' (2003) research shows that high expectations and home communications surrounding education are stronger influences on student learning overall.

Research shows that various cultural groups have different concepts of family engagement. Scholars have found that parents from different cultural groups such as Japanese, British, US American and Dutch (Netherlands) believe that parents are as accountable as teachers for their children's school success, especially in the primary or elementary years of schooling (Driessen *et al.*, 2005; Holloway *et al.*, 2008; Lau *et al.*, 2012). In the USA, recent changes made to federal education laws under the Every Student Succeeds Act (ESSA, 2016) places increased expectations on the part of schools to include parents in their children's education, making this work a national priority (US Department of Education, 2015). Section 1111 of ESSA (n.p.) states that local education agencies (or school districts across the USA) must now state *how* they will communicate with parents with the goal of 'lowering barriers to greater participation by parents in school planning, review, and improvement experienced.'

Depending on cultural norms and practices, some parents or caregivers may choose to support home learning or homework, monitor their child's academic progress and work with teachers to develop their child's academic skills. Other norms, however, differ cross-culturally and may reveal a 'teacher as expert' ideology, which parents would not violate. Epstein *et al.* (2001) developed a six-dimensional model as a framework for conceptualizing and supporting parental involvement. The various components include: (1) parenting – schools providing resources to help parents establish a positive home environment to foster children's development; (2) home–school communication – exchanges between home and school concerning children's development; (3) home learning activities – parents' involvement in various learning activities that take place at home; (4) volunteering at school – parents providing assistance to facilitate the school's functioning; (5) decision-making – parents collaborating with the school in making school management decisions; and (6) collaborating with the community – parents' identifying and using the available community resources for promoting children's learning and development. Epstein's framework, however, is grounded in a Western cultural model of education that encourages and builds home–school partnerships. Essentially, in multilingual settings there are likely widely diverse views of parental engagement and even various definitions of and approaches to education. A Western-based view of parental involvement may cause educators to believe that parents 'don't care' about their children's learning, when, in fact, the opposite may be true.

Other outcomes or 'indirect effects', beyond increased academic achievement, have been found (Keith *et al.*, 1986). For instance, children whose parents are in regular contact with schools feel more confident in their abilities to engage their child in school work or have higher expectations of their child. Grolnick and Slowiaczek (1994) proposed that children's attitudes and motivations related to school might also be influenced by parental involvement, which may result in positive outcomes related to children's academic achievement. Overall, based on the research, there appears to be a positive effect on children's attendance in school and students' graduation rates as a result of parental involvement or engagement (Epstein, 2001; Henderson & Mapp, 2002), and this positive effect occurs irrespective of race or language.

International research and literature on parent engagement

Goodall and Vorhaus (2010) conducted an extensive review of more than 1200 international articles on parental engagement. Their five-month review included identifying empirical research and reviews using key terms such as parent, engagement, pupil or student, achievement and community or family. The authors identified evidence-based literature on the types of activities that parents engaged in to support child learning. They found that, overall, the most effective practices that parents engaged in to support their child's learning was home-literacy practices where parents helped or taught their child in the home setting.

In their work on family engagement, Goodall and Montgomery (2014) describe a three-step continuum of parental involvement that ranges from a parent's involvement in schools on one end to parental engagement with a child's learning on the other end. The three steps along the continuum range from (1) parent involvement in school, where parents are physically present and active in traditional school-based activities; (2) parent involvement with schooling, where parents and schools exchange information either in the home or at the school; and (3) parent engagement, which has significant parental agency in a child's learning. Examples of step 3 – parental engagement with child learning – include parents providing supplemental education (tuition) for their child and/or taking a leadership role in school related events. The authors note that for parents to be 'most effective... engagement needs to be rooted in the home, in an attitude that fosters learning' (Goodall & Montgomery, 2014: 402). They further that

> by the third phase, it is clear that parents and schools share this responsibility. A shift in agency, has occurred, a movement to a more equitable situation, and one that previous literature has shown to be of positive value for children. (Goodall & Montgomery, 2014: 407)

While the shift in agency – that is, a shared responsibility for child learning – appears to support higher levels of student learning and academic outcomes, for multilingual families, this type of engagement may not only be linguistically incongruent, it may be culturally unfamiliar and uncomfortable. In short, with multilingual families, it is difficult to advance a one-size-fits-all approach to family engagement.

Although Western research is pervasive in the literature on family engagement, new research continues to emerge. For example, in a recent study conducted by Kim *et al.* (2017) examined urban Chinese parents' different orientations toward education participation based on being from 'poorer' or 'wealthier' homes. They analyzed surveys from 503 respondents and conducted interviews with about 60 individuals. In contrast to studies conducted in Western societies, where wealthier parents are more likely to have higher achieving children than those from poorer homes, this study found that 'poorer' children had superior study habits due to their 'strong achievement motivation and parents' involvement' (Kim *et al.*, 2017: 93). In other words, the authors found that children from low income backgrounds were more highly motivated to study and that their parents were more invested in their child's school success.

International research on parental involvement or engagement underscores Jeynes' (2003) finding above. For example, David *et al.* in Australia (1987 cited in Abd-El-Fattah, 2006) found that parental involvement predicted reading progress in a sample of Australian second graders who were followed from kindergarten. In the context of the Philippines and the USA, data collected and analyzed from 692 Philippines parents and 1410 US parents showed that among American parents, direct involvement at home (namely helping with homework in the home and reading books with children) yielded positive benefits for children's grade performance. In contrast, among Filipino parents, indirect forms of involvement, such as parents volunteering in school, were associated with higher grade performance (Lee Blair, 2014).

Rurality and Multilingual Families

Rurality

According to the United Nations (2017), nearly 46% of the world resides in rural settings. In the USA, federal guidelines reveal that about 19% of the population is rural, 71% is White, 13% Hispanic, 10% Black, 2% Asian, 2% American Indian and 2% two or more races. In the USA, almost a quarter of all students attend rural schools. Yet rurality itself is ambiguous with no internationally set definition of the geospatial designation. Documents from the UN note that the characteristics that distinguish urban from rural areas are 'not yet amenable to a single definition' (United Nations, 2017: n.p.).

Although labels such as rural and urban are frequently used in education to describe schools and the students within them, in reality these divisions are not as neat and clear as one might suppose. For example, imagine a community that is designated rural located on an island, and then imagine another rural community that is located on a high plains desert through which a high-speed rail stops regularly. Both may be considered rural based on distance to an urbanized setting, but the communities are very likely to differ in many ways, including access to local resources and community cultural norms and views. Hence, the concept of rurality must be fluid and dynamic rather than static in order to capture what happens within those geospaces.

John and Ford (2017: 3) describe the pervasive view that rurality is typically considered negative; yet, like urban settings, rurality itself remains 'ill defined'. The authors argue that 'the urban/rural binary was a colonial construct imposed on Native peoples through the conquest of the Americas' (John & Ford, 2017: 4). They suggest that rather than thinking of places as fixed categories with static characteristics scholars should attend to the *social processes* (italics retained from original) occurring within geographic spaces to understand the ways that people live, work and cooperate. Rural settings in general, like Indigenous settings in particular, can and do serve as 'epicenters' for resistance and collective being. I add that in rural settings, schools are spaces from which such social events, activities and community engagement processes can be activated and understood.

Thus, while in this book I use the term rural and rurality as terminology to capture some of the characteristics and social processes within geographic spaces, I recognize that the rural/urban binary is an artificial construct that is not well understood and that has been complicit in perpetuating deficit ideologies across groups of people. In addition, I recognize that social media and television, such as the popular television series *Ozark*, perpetuate images and stereotypes of people living in rural settings that need to be both unpacked and interrogated.

Rural settings present both challenges and opportunities for educators of multilingual students and families. To date and to our knowledge, most of the research on school–home connections and partnerships has focused on urban or suburban settings with little actual research conducted in rural settings themselves (Semke & Sheridan, 2012). However, at the same time, scholars infrequently identify their research as 'rural' per se, leaving suspect the actual quantity of research and work being conducted in rural settings. In this book, I consider rural spaces to be characterized as follows:

- sociohistorically and culturally rich;
- geographically isolated;
- have a strong sense of community;

[handwritten margin note: Many differences within rural settings.]

- have limited access to resources (financial, social and health related) to support students and families; and
- have teachers who may be un- or underprepared for linguistic diversity (Coady *et al.*, 2015; Semke & Sheridan, 2012; Terrazas & Fix, 2009) but committed to and participants in the community.

A recent trend in the USA is the settlement of immigrant multilingual families in 'new destination settings', that is, locations where multilingual children and families have not historically moved or settled (Suro & Singer, 2002). Those settings pose particular challenges for educators because they are frequently rural, semi-rural or nonurban settings, and teachers lack preparation to address the cultural and linguistic diversity of students and families (Lucas *et al.*, 2008).

Cicchinelli and Beesley (2017) state that approximately half of all school districts in the United States are classified as rural. In a recent analysis, Cicchinelli and Barley (2010) noted that the number one most frequently addressed issue in rural education are the factors (poverty of families, school resources, distance) that affect student performance, followed by the issue of teacher preparation and professional development. Rural teachers of multilingual children in our study underscore their concerns for resources (time and financial), that they feel are inequitably allocated to rural schools. They also feel the effects of poverty in rural schools on children's learning.

Rural schools and rural teacher education have undoubtedly been largely overlooked across the educational landscape (Arnold *et al.*, 2005; Glover *et al.*, 2016; Howley & Howley, 2004) but some promising research from rural education networks has emerged from Australia (Pegg, 2018) and from Canada (Corbett, 2014; Wallin, 2009). This research has focused on rural education and education disparities internationally (Pegg, 2018) or within Indigenous or First Nations students (Corbett, 2014). Similarly, a body of rural education research in the USA addresses English learners from the context of Indigenous students with little on immigrant English learners, an arguably distinct population within the rural EL community.

Research conducted internationally can contribute to current US-based research in understanding the complexities associated with rurality across different settings. For instance, the need to identify, prepare and retain teachers for rural schools is shared by international scholars (Corbett, 2014). Pegg (2018) describes how international test scores such as the Programme for International Student Assessment (PISA, 2018) can be disaggregated internationally by designation (urban, suburban, rural), demonstrating similar trends of low performance among rural students around the world. International alliances can build richer understandings of rural education across distinct settings, and some work is being conducted to support a network of scholars and teacher educators (ISFIRE, 2018).

However, not all international research can capture the localized knowledges embedded in rural schools. For example, within the USA, schools in rural California are very likely to be different from rural Idaho or rural Texas, where crop industries, contexts of reception (Stepick & Dutton Stepick, 2009), and migration networking can all affect rural multilingual families. Local economies and labor drive migration patterns, and schools are recipients of the effects of migration patterns. State level political policies on immigration, for instance, will also affect educational practices.

In their work with immigrant Latino families in the USA, Dondero and Muller (2012) found that language difference was an additional educational stratification between native English-speaking students and bilingual Latino students. In other words, rural schools offered fewer linguistic support services to multilinguals than those settling into established destinations. Within the USA, rural settings have seen growth in multilingual students by more than 200& in the southeast, midwest and northwest regions of the country (Suro & Singer, 2013). This geographic redistribution has presented challenges for educators where existing cultural norms and continuities.

As opposed to the fluid and dynamic definition of rurality proposed in this book, US National Center for Education Statistics' (NCES, 2006) guidelines and US Department of Education describe three types of rurality. The first, is *fringe* territories are those located five or less miles from an urbanized area. Second are *distant* territories that are located more than five miles, but less than 25 miles from an urbanized area. Finally, *remote* territories are those situated more than 25 miles from an urbanized area. Our work with rural schools in Florida has taken place in rural schools, and each school – even those within similar rural categories described here – function in different ways. I have found that the relationship between teachers in communities of practice, the role of the school principal, and the ways that schools welcome multilingual families has more of an effect on family engagement than does different categories of rurality (Table 1.1).

The different labels of rurality tend to mask the variation within rural settings and contribute to a false binary of rural–urban. In fact, even

Table 1.1 NCES (2006) subdefinitions of rurality

Rural

Fringe	Census-defined rural territory that is less than or equal to 5 miles from an urbanized area, as well as rural territory that is less than or equal to 2.5 miles from an urban cluster.
Distant	Census-defined rural territory that is more than 5 miles but less than or equal to 25 miles from an urbanized area, as well as rural territory that is more than 2.5 miles but less than or equal to 10 miles from an urban cluster.
Remote	Census-defined rural territory that is more than 25 miles from an urbanized area and is also more than 10 miles from an urban cluster.

'remote rural' settings, itself negatively positioned by its distance from an urbanized setting, cannot be considered a homogeneous space. Although most research related to rural education focuses on demographics and statistics related to student achievement and completion rates (Arnold *et al.*, 2005), some research on the experiences of rural teachers is beginning to emerge (Blair, 2017). Mainstream books such as the *Hillbilly Ellegy: A Memoir of a Family and Culture in Crisis* (Vance, 2016) have contributed to the rising attention paid on rural settings and their cultural and contextual differences. Blair (2017: 326), for example, writes, 'I quickly discovered that there was a richness and complexity to rural life that intersected with the urban experience, but yet, was completely different; a different place'.

The US-based National Rural Education Association (NREA, 2018) has identified some common challenges within rural settings, with the aim of scholars and teachers building a cohesive program to build rural education networks and identify solutions to problems within rural schools. The identified schools' need for the retention of teachers and preparation of specialized teachers for diverse students, in addition to adequate resources related to family engagement. Rural schools face geographic distance from resources, which acts as a barrier to providing educational, social and health support for children and families. For multilingual families, geographic distance also limits access to interpreters and translators, exacerbating communication difficulties for children and families in terms of educational needs and school–home interaction. Related to physical isolation is the social isolation that accompanies distance. Families are unable to network socially or identify shared solutions to challenges such as day care for young children or access to medical facilities. Social networking among families is difficult and infrequent (Stacciarini *et al.*, 2011).

Yet rural settings can also become sites as 'epicenters' of resistance in the context of Indigenous education (John & Ford, 2017); communities (Whitlock, 2017); and continuity of education. Referring to the contributions of rural settings on education, Blair notes,

> there was an acknowledgement of the difficulties attached to rural life, but simultaneously, there was an honouring of the family/community traditions, history, values and beliefs that have defined their lives. Most parents had attended and played sports, in the same schools their children now attended. There was a continuity to this experience, and despite challenges to the adequacy of the schools, parents often don't want anything to change. (Blair, 2017: 326)

Conclusion

This chapter has overviewed some key concepts for educators who work or will work with multilingual children and families in rural educational settings. Some of the key concepts include the nature of immigration and migration on a worldwide scale in today's 21st century global environment; definitions of parent involvement and family engagement, linguistic and cultural diversity of families; and challenges and contributions of multilingual families in rural settings. In subsequent chapters of this book, I explore those challenges and opportunities in depth, and share experiences and suggestions for educators working with multilingual families and students.

Activities

Activity 1

Create a Venn diagram with three circles (Figure 1.4). Complete the diagram using three key terms: migrant, immigrant, refugee. Based on information provided in this chapter, what general characteristics overlap among these three groups? What are some key factors that affect schooling for children who represent one of these groups?

Activity 2

Search online for international NGOs that assist international migrants. What are some of the activities they engage in? What are the main needs of the population they serve? How does their work intersect with education in today's global environment?

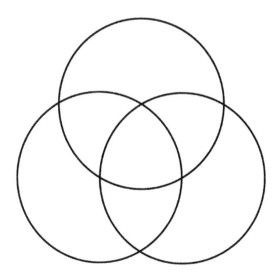

Figure 1.4 Venn diagram

Activity 3

Watch the TED Talk about Malala Yousafzai by her father. What cultural barriers existed for Malala and her father? What value for education did Malala's father project? How has Malala's view of education changed over time?

TED Talk: My Daughter Malala (Ziauddin Yousafzai) (16'32')
https://www.ted.com/talks/ziauddin_yousafzai_my_daughter_malala

Activity 4

Access the NREA's website (see https://www.nrea.net/) and their research agenda for 2016–2021. Which of their 10 research priorities seem most pressing to you and your school? How might you rank the priorities for your school?

References

Abd-El-Fattah, SM. (2006) The relationship among Egyptian adolescents' perception of parental involvement, academic achievement, and achievement goals: A mediational analysis. *International Education Journal* 7 (4), 499–509.

American Community Survey (2014) US Census Bureau. See https://www.census.gov/programs-surveys/acs/.

Arnold, M.L., Newman, J.H., Gaddy, D.D. and Dean, C.B. (2005) A look at the condition of rural education research: Setting a direction for future research. *Journal of Research in Rural Education* 20 (6), 1–25.

Blair, E.J. (2017) Teaching in the country: A critical analysis of the experiences of rural teachers in the United States and Jamaica. In W.M. Reynolds (ed.) *Forgotten Places: Critical Studies in Rural Education* (pp. 323–340). New York: Peter Lang.

Ceballo, R., Maurizi, L.K., Suarez, G.A. and Aretakis, M.T. (2014) Gift and sacrifice: Parental involvement in Latino adolescents' education. *Cultural Diversity & Ethnic Minority Psychology* 20 (1), 116–127.

Central Broadcasting Station (CBS) (2010) 'Harvest of Shame' 50 years later. See https://www.cbsnews.com/news/harvest-of-shame-50-years-later/.

Cicchinellli, L.F. and Barley, Z. (2010) Sustaining coherent reform: An evaluation guide for districts and schools. ERIC Document ED544260. See https://eric.ed.gov/?id=ED544260

Cicchinelli, L.F. and Beesley, A.D. (2017) Introduction: Current state of the science in rural education research In G.C. Nugent, G.M. Kunz, S.M. Sheridan, T.A. Glover and L.L. Knoche (eds.) *Rural Education Research in the United States* (pp. 1–14). Switzerland: Springer International.

Coady, M. (2009) *"Solamente libros importantes"*: Literacy practices and ideologies of migrant farmworking families in north central Florida. In G. Li (Ed.) *Multicultural Families, Home Literacies and Mainstream Schooling* (pp. 113–128). Charlotte, NC: New Age.

Coady, M. and Ariza, E. (2010) Struggling for meaning and identity (and a passing grade): High-stakes writing in English as a second language. *MEXTESOL* 34 (1), 11–27.

Coady, M.R., Coady, T.J. and Nelson, A. (2015) Assessing the needs of immigrant, Latino families and teachers in rural settings: Building home-school partnerships. *NABE*

Journal of Research and Practice, (6). See https://www2.nau.edu/nabej-p/ojs/index.php/njrp/article/view/42

Coady, M., Harper, C. and de Jong, E. (2016) Aiming for equity: Preparing mainstream teachers for inclusion or inclusive classrooms? *TESOL Quarterly* 50 (2), 340–368. DOI: 10.1002/tesq.223

Coady, M., Makalela, L. and Lopez, M. (2019, in review) Metaliteracy development and writing among 4th grade multilingual students in South Africa.

Corbett, M. (2014) Toward a geography of rural education in Canada. *Canadian Journal in Education* 37 (3), 1–22.

Datta, P. (2004) The push-pull factors of undocumented migration from Bangladesh to West Bengal: A perception study. *Qualitative Report* 9 (2), 335–358, ERIC document EJ848371. See http://nsuworks.nova.edu/tqr/vol9/iss2/9/.

Deslandes, R., Royer, E., Turcotte, D. and Bertrand, R. (1997) School achievement at the secondary level: Influence of parenting style and parent involvement in schooling. *McGill Journal of Education* 32, 191–207.

Dondero, M. and Muller, C. (2012) A scientific medium of social study and interpretation. *Social Forces* 9 (2), 477–502. See https://www.ncbi.nlm.nih.gov/pmc/articles/PMC3724212/#SOS127C45.

Driessen, G., Smit, F. and Sleegers, P. (2005) Parental involvement and educational achievement. *British Educational Research Journal* 32 (4), 509–532.

Edgell, P. and Docka, D. (2007) Beyond the nuclear family? Familism and gender ideology in diverse religious commuities. *Sociological Forum* 22 (1), 26–51. DOI: 10.1111/j.1573-7861.2006.00003.x

Epstein, J. (2001) *School, Family and Community Partnerships.* Boulder, CO: Westview Press.

European Commission (2012) Europeans and their languages. See http://ec.europa.eu/commfrontoffice/publicopinion/index.cfm/Survey/getSurveyDetail/search/languages/surveyKy/1049.

Ferlazzo, L. (2009) Family literacy, English language learners, and parent engagement. *Library Media Connection,* 28 (1), 20–21.

Fernández, E. and López, G. R. (2017) When parents behave badly: a critical policy analysis of parental involvement in schools. In M.D. Young and S. Diem (eds) *Critical Approaches to Education Policy Analysis: Moving Beyond Tradition* (pp. 111–130). New York, NY: Springer.

García, O. (2016) *Translanguaging with Multilingual Students: Learning from Classroom Moments.* New York: Routledge.

Glover, T.A., Nugent, G.C., Chumney, F.L., Ihlo, T., Shapiro, E.S., Guard, K., Koziol, N. and Bovaird, J. (2016) Investigating rural teachers' professional development, instructional knowledge, and classroom practice. *Journal of Research in Rural Education* 31 (3), 1–16.

Goodall, J. and Montgomery, C. (2014) Parental involvement to parental engagement: A continuum. *Educational Review* 66 (4), 399–410.

Goodall, J. and Vorhaus, J. (2010) *Review of Best Practice in Parental Engagement.* Department for Education, UK.

Grolnick, W.S. and Slowiaczek, M.L. (1994) Parents' involvement in children's schooling: A multidimensional conceptualization and motivational model. *Child Development* 65, 237–252.

Habermehl, W.H. (2006) Helping Latino parents navigate the education system. *Leadership,* 35 (4), 24–25.

Henderson, A. and Mapp, K. (2002) *A New Wave of Evidence: The Impact of School, Family and Community Connections on Student Achievement.* Austin, TX: National Center for Family and Community Connections with Schools.

Hill, N.E. and Tyson, D.F. (2009) Parental involvement in middle school: A meta-analytic assessment of the strategies that promote achievement. *Developmental Psychology* 45, 740–763.

Holloway, S.D., Yamamoto, Y., Suzuki, S. and Mindnich, J.D. (2008) Determinants of parental involvement in early schooling: Evidence from Japan. *Early Childhood Research & Practice* (ECRP) 10 (1), 1–22.

Hornby, G. and Witte, C. (2010) Parent involvement in inclusive primary schools in New Zealand: Implications for improving practice and for teacher education. *School Psychology International* 31 (5), 495–508.

Howley, A. and Howley, C.B. (2004, December) *High Quality Teaching: Providing for Rural Teachers' Professional Development.* An AEL policy brief. Charleston, WV: AEL.

Hutchins, D.J., Greenfeld, M.D., Epstein, J.L., Sanders, M.G. and Galindo, C. (2012) *Multicultural Partnerships: Involve all Families.* Larchmont, NY: Eye on Education.

International Rescue Committee (2017) See https://www.rescue.org/.

International Symposium for Innovation in Rural Education (ISFIRE) (2018) See http://www.montana.edu/crre/isfire2018/.

Jeynes, W.H. (2003). A meta-analysis: The effects of parental involvement on minority children's academic achievement. *Education and Urban Society* 35 (2), 202–218.

John, K.D. and Ford, D.R. (2017) The rural is nowhere: Bringing Indigeneity and urbanism into educational research. In W.M. Reynolds (ed.) *Forgotten Places: Critical Studies in Rural Education* (pp. 3–14). New York: Peter Lang.

Keith, T.Z., Reimers, T.M., Fehrmann, P.G., Pottebaum, S.M. and Aubey, L.W. (1986) Parental involvement, homework, and TV time: Direct and indirect effects on high school achievement. *Journal of Educational Psychology* 78, 373–380.

Kim, S.W, Brown, K., Kim, E.J. and Fong, V.L. (2017) 'Poorer children study better': How urban Chinese young adults perceive relationships between wealth and academic achievement. *Comparative Education Review* 62 (1), 84–102.

Kress, G. (2009) *Multimodality: A Social Semiotic Approach to Contemporary Communication.* New York, NY: Routledge.

Lau, E.H., Li, H. and Rao, N. (2012) Exploring parental involvement in early years education in China: Development and validation of the Chinese Early Parental Involvement Scale (CEPIS). *International Journal Of Early Years Education* 20 (4), 405–421.

Lee Blair, S. (2014) Parental involvement and children's educational performance: A comparison of Filipino and U.S. parents. *Journal of Comparative Family Studies* 45 (3), 351–366.

Li, S. and Luo, W. (2017) Creating a translanguaging space for high school emergent bilinguals. *CATESOL Journal* 29 (2), 139–162.

Li, Z., Chu, C-C. and Coady, M. (2014) The transformative power of gaming literacy: What can we learn from adolescent English language learners' literacy engagement in World of Warcraft (WoW)? In H. Gerbera and S. Abrams (eds) *Bridging Literacies with Videogames* (pp. 129–154). Rotterdam: Sense Publishers.

Lopez, G. (2001) The value of hard work: Lessons on parent involvement from an (im) migrant household. *Harvard Educational Review* 71 (3), 416–438.

Lopez, M. and Coady, M. (2018) Mother tongue education in the Philippines. *Proceedings from the Third Conference on Multilingual Literacies and Education.* Johannesburg, South Africa.

Lucas, T., Villegas, A.M. and Freedson-Gonzalez, M. (2008) Linguistically responsive teacher education: Preparing classroom teachers to teach English language learners. *Journal of Teacher Education*, 59, 361–373. doi 10.1177/0022487108322110

Luna, T. (2012) How a penny made me feel like a millionaire. TED talk. See https://www.ted.com/talks/tania_luna_how_a_penny_made_me_feel_like_a_millionaire.

Makalela, L. (2015) Bilingualism in South Africa: Reconnecting with *Ubuntu* translanguaging. In O. García and A. Lin (eds) *Encyclopedia of Bilingualism and Bilingual Education* (pp. 297–309). New York: Springer.

Makalela, L. (2016) *Not Eleven Languages: Mutual Inter-comprehensibility and New Multilingual Practices in Post-apartheid South Africa*. New York: Mouton De Gruyter.

Miedel, W.T. and Reynolds, A.J. (1999) Parent involvement in early intervention for disadvantaged children: Does it matter? *Journal of School Psychology* 37, 379–402.

Migration Policy Institute (2015) Net number of migration by country, 1950–2015 (by five-year intervals). See http://www.migrationpolicy.org/programs/data-hub/maps-immigrants-and-emigrants-around-world.

Migration Policy Institute (2017) Immigrant and emigrant populations by origin and destination. See http://www.migrationpolicy.org/programs/data-hub/international-migration-statistics.

Miliband, D. (2017) The refugee crisis is a test of our character. TED talk. See https://www.ted.com/talks/david_miliband_the_refugee_crisis_is_a_test_of_our_character.

National Center for Education Statistics (NCES) (2006) Definitions of rurality. See https://nces.ed.gov/surveys/ruraled/definitions.asp

National Rural Education Association (NREA) (2018) Research agenda 2016–2021. See https://www.nrea.net/Research_and_Publications.

Niemeyer, A.E., Wong, M.M., and Westerhaus, K.J. (2009) Parental involvement, *familismo*, and academic performance in Hispanic and Caucasian adolescents. *North American Journal of Psychology* 11 (3), 613–631.

Pegg, J. (2018). *Strengthening Rural Education: Alternatives in Enhancing Education in Rural Areas*. Presentation at the International Symposium For Innovation in Rural Education (ISIRE). Bozeman, MT.

Programme for International Student Assessment (2018) PISA test. OECD. See http://www.oecd.org/pisa/.

Sabogal, F., Marín, G., Otero-Sabogal, R., Marín, B. and Perez-Stable, E.J. (1987) Hispanic familism and acculturation: What changes and what doesn't? *Hispanic Journal of Behavioral Sciences* 9, 397–412.

Salinas, C. and Fránquiz, M.E. (2004) *Scholars in the Field: The Challenges of Migrant Education*. AEL Publishing.

Semke, C.A. and Sheridan, S.M. (2012) Family-school connections in rural educational settings: A systematic review of the empirical literature. *School Community Journal*, 22 (1), 21–48.

Shumow, L. and Miller, J.D. (2001) Parents' at-home and at-school academic involvement with young adolescents. *Journal of Early Adolescence* 21, 68–91.

Singer, A. (2004) *The Rise of New Immigrant Gateways*. In Living Cities Census Series. Washington, DC: The Brookings Institution.

Stacciarini, J.M., Wiens, B., Coady, M., Schwait, A., Pérez, A., Locke, B., LaFlam, M., Page, V. and Bernardi, K. (2011) CBPR: Building partnerships with Latinos in rural areas for a wellness approach to mental health. *Issues in Mental Health Nursing Journal* 32 (8), 486–492.

Stepick, A. and Dutton Stepick, C. (2009) Contexts of reception and feelings of belonging. *Forum: Qualitative Social Research* 10 (3), Art 15. See http://www.qualitative-researchnet/index.php/fqs/article/view/1366/2862.

Suro, R. and Singer, A. (2002) *Latino Growth in Metropolitan America: Changing Patterns, New Locations*. Washington, DC: The Brookings Institution.

Taniguchi, K. and Hirakawa, Y. (2015) Dynamics of community participation, student achievement and school management: The case of primary schools in a rural area of Malawi. *Compare: A Journal of Comparative and International Education* 46 (3), 479–502.

Terrazas A. and Fix, M. (2009) *The Binational Option: Meeting the Instructional Needs of Limited English Proficient Students*. Washington, DC: Migration Policy Institute.

United Nations (UN) (2017) Population density and urbanization. See https://unstats.un.org/unsd/demographic/sconcerns/densurb/densurbmethods.htm.

US Department of Education (2015) Every Student Succeeds Act of 2015. See https://www. ed.gov/essa?src=rn.

US Department of Education (2018) Migrant education. See https://www2.ed.gov/ programs/mep/index.html.

Vance, J. D. (2016) *Hillbilly Elegy: Memoir of a Family and Culture in Crisis.* New York: Harper.

Vocke, K.S. (2007) *Where Do I Go from Here?: Meeting the Unique Educational Needs of Migrant Students.* New York: Heinemann.

Wallin, D.C. (2009) Rural education: A review of provincial and territorial initiatives. *Manitoba Education Citizenship and Youth.* See https://www.edu.gov.mb.ca/k12/ docs/reports/rural_ed/rural_ed_final.pdf.

Whitlock, R.U. (2017) A memoir of Littleville School: Identity, community, and rural education in a curriculum study of rural space. In W.M. Reynolds (ed.) *Forgotten Places: Critical Studies in Rural Education* (pp. 169–188). New York: Peter Lang.

Zimmerman-Orozco, S. (2011) A circle of caring. *Educational Leadership* 68 (8), 64–68.

2 Framing the Issues: A 'Strengths-Based Approach' to Family Engagement

Highlights

- A strengths-based approach to family engagement.
- Family and educator voices.
- A framework for educators.
  - Linguistically-responsive pedagogy for family engagement.
  - Freire: Critical consciousness, *conscientização* and praxis.
- Relational trust and care.
- Activities for further learning.

Real Scenario

Jackie is a 5th grade primary school teacher enrolled in an online teacher professional development (PD) program for educators of English learner students in a rural school district in the USA. The first course she takes in her program is called 'Guided Inquiry', a course in which she must identify key problems of educational practice and ways investigate those problems to find solutions that support her students' learning. The online discussions in the course are virtual (online) spaces for educators to share their experiences and to develop an 'inquiry stance' (Dana & Yendol-Hoppey, 2014). An inquiry stance is an orientation to teaching in which teachers reflect upon and ask questions about their practice and student learning. Jackie reads through the online course materials and pauses on the proverbial 'pink elephant in the room'. No one, it seems to her, wants to talk about equity issues between the English speaking and the non-English speaking students in her district. For that matter nor does she.

Jackie writes on the course discussion board, 'Advocating social jus-tice is probably the least important passion for me at this time. I think that it is less important because it is not something that I can identify with.... I believe the underlying reason that I am not passionate about [social jus-tice] is because there is a political side to it as well and I do not like any-thing to do with politics. Some examples that come to mind are LGBTR [sic] rights, gender bathrooms and abortion. Again, I am not saying that these issues are not important, it is just that they are a not as important to me as other issues like bullying or more options and help for lower socio-economic students.'

Introduction

As described in Chapter 1, family engagement with schools is an essential aspect of student learning, yet surprisingly there remain multiple challenges to building strong relationships with multilingual families, despite research that shows that family engagement supports student learning (Jeynes, 2003) and federal guidelines mandate it. Some of the challenges to family engagement with rural multilingual families include linguistically responsive communication to families, which may be exac-erbated by three main factors: (1) linguistic and cultural differences between schools and homes; (2) the rural nature of communities that limits physical interaction and relationship-building activities between schools and homes; and (3) limited resources of rural settings and the associated need to prepare teachers for multilingual families.

This chapter describes these characteristics (language, rurality and resources) and then focuses on the strengths and opportunities that are garnered by working with rural multilingual families. To do this, we must shift our *pedagogical lens* through which we view family engagement. By pedagogical lens I refer not only to specific practices related to teaching and learning, but also the wide-angle view taken by educators when work-ing with students and families, and how we become learners as well as teachers. To change our lens from challenges to opportunities, I use the work of two important educators who have contributed to our under-standing of pedagogy: Gloria Ladson-Billings and Paulo Freire. Together, I review the contributions of these educators and their influence on edu-cational practices to rural schools.

In this chapter, I describe a strengths-based approach to working with multilingual families. I delineate what multilingual, immigrant families have to say about the challenges that they face when interacting with schools, as well as what educators view as challenges to working with those same families. I then frame this work with a critical lens by describing culturally and linguistically-responsive pedagogy based on the work of several key scholars. We build upon that framework by exploring critical consciousness or *conscientização*, which was described by Freire. I discuss the importance of trust and care, which are essential features of family engagement. Finally, I propose a model of family engagement that will be further clarified and described in Chapters 4 and 5 of the book.

A Strengths-Based Approach to Family Engagement: Linguistic and Cultural Difference as Educational Resources

Multilingual families are a tremendously diverse resource in communities around the world. The way that families function, their unique oral and written communication patterns, their cultural and traditional family rituals and practices, and family members' roles all influence the way children enter and orient themselves to school. From the outset, multilingualism is a resource that is grossly undervalued around the world (Ruiz, 1984) and under-investigated in the context of education (Coady & Yilmaz, 2017). Yet connecting language and literacy practices between the home and school is essential in the languages and literacy development of children. In fact, Weiss notes that there is 'a skyscraper of research that supports the fact that family engagement is one of, if not the strongest predictor, of what happens to children' (Weiss, 2014: n.p.). Consider the scenario below.

The Álvarez family lives in a rural agricultural setting in a southern US state (Coady, 2009). The Álvarez parents have five children, one of whom was born in an Indigenous region of Mexico. The home oral language of communication among the family members shifts regularly between Spanish, which was the language of schooling of the parents, English, which is the language of schooling of all five children, and Otomí, an Indigenous language of Mexico spoken in the central high planes (*altiplano*) region. Each of the Álvarez parents attended school until the 8th grade, which is considered the *primaria*, or primary level schooling. However, the parents could not continue to attend school because of the distance and cost associated with traveling to a secondary school. As is the case in many countries around the world, secondary schooling costs Mexican families money for books and supplies, which is beyond the reach of many rural families.

As a young couple, the Álvarez parents immigrated to the USA in search of labor for themselves and opportunities for their children. Prior to moving, the Álvarezes worked with their own parents as craftspeople who produced hand embroidered *mantelas*, or tablecloths, and other woven fabric products representative of the local culture. Although they speak virtually no English, the parents attend every school function and event at each of their children's schools. They confess that they sit in the back of the room so that no one asks them questions in English, which would embarrass their children. They attend because they want to show support for their children's education, and they feel limited and ashamed that they cannot help their children do homework in English at night.

The Álvarez family attends religious services each Sunday at a church that is about an hour and a half drive from their home. They drive this distance each week because the church service there is in Spanish and all of their family members can understand Spanish. The liturgy is given in Spanish and the church's written materials are in Spanish. So although the Álvarez children have never had any formal instruction in Spanish, they are able to decode and understand written Spanish to various degrees. In the home, however, the religious materials, which the parents brought with them a decade earlier from Mexico, are written in Otomí. The children cannot read Otomí, but the parents can read the Bible in that language to them and they can understand oral Otomí.

The religious language and literacy practices in the Álvarez home parallel those of their family traditions. Señora Álvarez, for example, safekeeps family recipes in several languages and she follows the recipes when she prepares traditional foods, particularly during holidays. Her interactions with her three daughters, whom she teaches to cook traditional foods, alternates between Otomí and Spanish. Written literacy such as the dated cloth calendar in Otomí from 2004 hanging from the wall in the living room reminds Señora Álvarez of local Mexican cultural events and people dressed in local costumes from the *altiplano* region.

The scenario above provides some beginning insight into the family's languages and literacy practices. Those languages and literacy practices are essential, as they reveal the cultural traditions, knowledges and practices of the family, the roles of the family members and the literacy resources to support the children's learning.

As an educator, *all* of the information presented above is essential to know in order to work most effectively with and to make sound instructional decisions for the Álvarez children and parents. Based on what we know about the family, the parents value education and want to support their children. The parents not only attend school functions as a display of their academic support, they also demonstrate the value of education and underscore the importance of family or *familismo*.

The Álvarez parents have linguistic and cultural differences that educators need to know and that may appear to be in conflict with what schools prioritize. How can educators communicate with the family? How can they convey information such as graduation procedures, the cultural expectations to volunteer in school or the results of student standardized testing? How can parents express their need for interpreters at school events and obtain information about their children's school events?

Although these issues seem like challenges, there are many ways for educators to reframe these challenges as opportunities to learn about the cultural and linguistic backgrounds of their students, to engage families, and to build the cultural and linguistic resources in the school and community. Moreover, educators who understand how multilingual family function, use language and literacy, are far better equipped to make instructional decisions for multilingual students. For example, when educators know the ways in which parents communicate with their children (the languages and literacies, the support structure and the roles), they are better able to connect and support student learning. In short, educators must be prepared to bridge both the linguistic and cultural differences between schools and families.

To conceptualize our work with multilingual families, I draw upon a 'strengths-based' orientation to building partnerships with multilingual families. I view the linguistic and cultural practices of families as resources that they bring to the school environment and are too often invisible to educators. Those resources reflect the realities of how languages are used around the world today, as described in Chapter 1, as well as the ways in which multilingual families perceive, 'know' and interact in the world (Kisthardt, 2012; Saleebey, 2012). A strengths-based orientation is an approach to building relationships that is person-centered, affirming and dynamic. It is *person-centered* because it recognizes that language and communication are essential to building relationships and being human, and communication occurs between people; it is *affirming* because this approach recognizes that multiple languages are resources that individuals draw upon for functioning and well-being, and that language is one aspect of individual and group identity; and it is *dynamic* because languages themselves are fluid, changing, and serve to illuminate the experiences and viewpoints of their speakers. This approach requires that educators explore their families' and students' strengths (Kisthardt, 2012), capabilities and functioning (Saleebey, 2012).

In the context of multilingual families, a strengths-based approach can be applied to the linguistic resources of the family, the way that the family interacts as a unit and its functioning in broader social settings such as a school. Some of the strengths of multilingual families include their histories, their traditional and cultural knowledges, skills and habits; their language and literacy practices; their social network and survival skills (Moll *et al.*, 1992); and their contributions to the communities in which they live and participate. In this regard, the languages and cultures of the families are resources upon which educators draw for student learning, fostering learning environments that are caring and support the well-being of the students. Teachers and educators who subscribe to a strengths-based orientation of multilingual families see families' languages, experiences and backgrounds as resources for teaching and learning – brought purposefully and directly into the classroom setting – rather than deficits that should be ignored or eradicated under monolingual language policies.

For example, in his seminal educational research connecting families and schools, Moll *et al.* (1992) describe how Latino families' knowledges were used in educational settings. Using a framework of 'funds of knowledge', they identified how the survival skills, cross-national travel and international experiences, and networking skills of Latino, immigrant families contributed to community wells or 'funds' of expertise. 'Funds of knowledge' also include the deep well of cultural and linguistic knowledge, such as home literacy practices, oral storytelling, religious and familial practices, and international travel and communication (Coady, 2009). In their work in the southwest USA, Moll *et al.* (1992) demonstrated how teachers in the community connected with families by investigating how families functioned and survived. The teachers subsequently utilized that information as a foundation for further student learning by inviting parents or caregivers, extended family members and other community members to share their knowledge and skills in the classroom. As in Moll and colleagues' funds of knowledge framework, individual family and student resources can be used in the classroom setting when educators acknowledge those skills and act upon that knowledge by connecting school and learning to the students' background (Moll *et al.*, 1992; Ruiz, 1984).

Family and educator voices

A strengths-based orientation of multilingual families, however, does not mask the reality that forming relationships between the home and school is not simple. Parents and caregivers hold views about education based on their own personal educational histories and experiences. For example, parents or caregivers who have graduated from 8th grade *primaria*, like the Álvarez parents, have different educational experiences from parents who completed a university degree. And caregivers who have had positive experiences in their own education often convey those messages to their children. Other experiences may not have been affirming of home languages, literacies and cultural practices. Some multilingual families believe erroneously that in order to 'get ahead' in the global environment, they must shed their home languages and cultures, use only the dominant social language and follow mainstream cultural practices. This paradigm is backwards, because language learning for multilingual students builds upon prior language knowledge (García, 2009). Moreover, deficit ideologies reinforce social inequities that tell multilingual families that their languages and who they are do not matter. Educators can be informed about the educational histories of their students and how parents or caregivers convey expectations about education to their child. It is our imperative as educators to challenge these deficit views and to identify local school-based practices to change them.

In my work in rural school districts with multilingual families, I have partnered with community agencies that provide social and health related services in Latino communities. Some of their work over the years included preparing *promotoras de salud*, or lay healthcare workers who are trained to become local experts and resources within the community, bilingual guides to community resources, and *fotonovelas* or graphic novels that demonstrate how multilingual families network and identify solutions to school-related topics such as attending the family engagement nights with teacher conferencing. In this context, families' histories and experiences in the community are invisible teachers in schools and teachers express similar frustration because they do not know how build relationships with families.

Our community partner asked multilingual families and educators about the challenges that they face when working rural schools. Below is a list of items that we compiled, based on informal interviews and conversations with educators and families.

Challenges that educators say they face when working with multilingual families

- Making them (multilingual parents and caregivers) not be fearful of coming to school for conferences or school events.
- Fear of school reporting them as illegal or undocumented.
- Families are constantly changing contact information; difficulty maintaining contact with them.
- Language and culture barriers. We struggle to get families that trust us.
- Fear of the school environment and a sense of inability to help their offspring.
- Fear of deportation (for undocumented families).
- How to make connections.
- Predetermined misconceptions of one another and language barriers.
- Lack of interpreters.
- Locating previous health and educational records.
- Communication barriers.
- Getting to know families and their backgrounds.
- Communication.
- Educational expectations.
- Threat of being deported is affecting students in the classroom.
- Fear of being different, not being accepted and fear of their immigrant status.
- Sociopolitical context.
- If the parents do not speak English, I cannot communicate concerns I have for their child.

Overall, educators view language and cultural differences as their main challenges to engaging families in schools. Educators' concerns reflect their own comfort-level regarding their ability to outreach to students and families in and outside of the school environment. Many of the statements above relate to linguistic and cultural differences, which educators view as 'barriers', 'misconceptions' and 'difficulties'. These reflect teachers' awareness of the social-emotional concerns of fear and isolation that multilingual families experience. In addition, in this context the issue of immigration and the social status of families was also repeated in educators' statements.

For their part, families also face challenges that prevent them from engaging with teachers, albeit different from those that teachers express. The following are statements from multilingual families, about half of who were immigrants in the community.

Challenges that rural multilingual families say they face

- Difficulty supporting my child's education.
- Feeling safe.
- Not being able to communicate with people in my new community.
- Trust.
- Anxiety.
- Fear of deportation and child left abandoned. Also, not being prepared or having a plan to deal with immigration issues.
- Providing for family on substandard or intermittent pay.
- Not knowing whom to trust.
- Lack of knowledge about transportation.
- Financial concerns.
- Having consistent employment.
- Providing essentials (food, clothes and medical).
- Lack of transportation, stable jobs, money.
- Lack of education ourselves.
- Lack of transportation (repeated by another adult).
- Inability to find resources that are friendly to our needs.
- Having to have kids translate at the store, doctor, school.
- Income.
- Exclusion.
- Economic difficulties.
- Language.

Families' challenges and concerns revealed practical issues of access to financial resources and work, transportation, language and immigration. Families in our partner, rural community sought to secure consistent work in order to provide household income. The rural nature of the community also meant that transportation (or lack thereof) was a major concern and a barrier to attending school events. It is easy, then, to see that the multilingual families have different priorities and challenges than the educators. These challenges made it difficult for parents to be available for school functions. For their part, the cultural orientation and background of the families underscore their view of schools in which teachers provide the primary support for student learning. Parents saw their role as attending to work and providing financial stability, transportation and healthcare. Importantly, the area where both educators and families expressed challenges was in their communication between the home and school.

The Rural Nature of Communities

The rural nature of schools necessarily means that there are challenges to the actual physical presence of families in schools and to relationship-building process between schools and homes. However, there are also some great advantages to rural settings. As Witte and Sheridan (2011: 3) describe,

> Rural schools are uniquely positioned to foster and benefit from family-school partnerships. Because of their centrality within the community, rural schools routinely connect with families in multiple capacities as part of typical daily routines... In many rural communities, the local school building is a point of pride for the community and houses sporting and cultural events, civic activities, and shelter during severe weather. Teachers serve as coaches and club sponsors which means that they have frequent and varied contact with students at multiple age and academic levels and their families.

For their part, educators in rural settings recognize the geographic and social isolation that both they faced and that their multilingual families experienced, although in different ways. For example, families need transportation to get to schools at times that are convenient for their varied works schedules. They also require interpreters, translators or school staff who speak their languages and understand their home cultures.

Domínguez (2017) describes this as 'ontological distance', which he defines as the 'dehumanizing distancing between subjects that emerges from uninterrrogated colonality' (2017: 226). Ontology refers to the nature of one's being; hence, ontological distance is the social, cultural and linguistic space that exists between minoritized students and families and those that represent a mainstream, nonminoritized identity. Ontological distance can be invisible, through unexamined beliefs and attitudes toward minoritized students, in white school curricula and in the expectations of parents from monolingual norms. Flores and Rosa (2015) interrogate this construct further by describing how ideologies about language are racialized. They describe how a white speaking norm and white listening norm establish expectations about how multilinguals are expected to communicate.

These ideas and needs are echoed above in the statements made early by multilingual families and educators. In addition to the invisible ontological distance that rural multilingual families experience, physical, geographic distance makes it challenging for families to attend school functions on a regular basis. This is not only due to lack of transportation, but also due to the costs associated with transportation such as gasoline, wear on tires and the automobile, and the time it takes to either drive or walk to school events. Too often there is an expectation that rural multilingual families participate as white monolinguals do. To be clear, the construct of a white monolingual norm is itself fraught with stereotyping, essentializing whiteness and masquerading diversity, yet it continues to distance the identities of multilingual families from schools.

In today's seemingly ubiquitous internet-based communication, I increasingly see schools propose that all families access school notes, documents, grades, homework and announcements online via the internet. Although this seems like a simple solution, this rarely works with rural multilingual families. In rural settings, access to the internet is either not available, or its service limited or unstable. In addition, families living in high poverty settings may run out of money mid-month on their phone service and are unable to access either phone or internet services. When they are able to pay, they may need new phone numbers and a new service provider.

Rural multilingual families we work with state that they prefer to know teachers personally rather than receive materials and information that they cannot understand, either for language or for cultural reasons. For instance, asking families to read bedtime stories to their children is not a traditional night-time event in many multilingual families' homes, and families may not have access to print reading materials or time to read. Moreover, families may not have access to online information, because the high cost of technology, internet and equipment is beyond their financial reach. When families are able to access online information, it is too often provided in a language that they do not understand. For example, today, more and more schools utilize parent portals and online school websites to convey grades, school calendars, attendance, events and even graduation information to parents. Assuming that all families have consistent access to information from the school is essential. These challenges to communication for rural, multilingual families are ever-present. However, teachers and educators have the opportunity to first know who families are personally and to use that knowledge to align educational practice to families' resources and strengths.

A Framework for Educators

In the opening scenario of this chapter, Jackie held a strong view of what she felt comfortable and not comfortable discussing with her colleagues in her online forum. While she wanted to support her multilingual students, she could not see the relationship between advocating for multilingual students and issues of social justice and equity. Her views underscore what educators often experience in their teacher education program: a focus on social justice issues without corresponding techniques, strategies and skills to address social justice issues (Cochran-Smith *et al.*, 2009). Moreover, Jackie specifically sought to avoid discussion of politics in the context of education, a stance I hear repeated frequently among educators who feel that education and politics need to remain separate.

This real scenario plays out repeatedly across schools where teachers and educators are provided annual professional development (PD) opportunities that focus on methodologies, teaching strategies, data-driven instruction and student achievement data. Those tend to further segregate multilingual students and families because of their overemphasis on traditional assessments and school curricula that focus only on student learning outcomes as goals of PD. The challenge for 21st-century education is to prepare educators to work with multilingual families by equipping them with skills and strategies that build upon families' ontologies, strengths such as migration networks, and that follow a social justice and equity framework. In other words, educators with a social justice and equity lens need to engage rural multilingual families.

Unfortunately, some common descriptors of multilingual students persist in education. Multilingual students are often described as:

- historically at risk for educational failure;
- limited [English] proficient;
- disadvantaged;
- underperforming;
- confused;
- non-non;
- none-none;
- illiterate;
- semiliterate; and
- double nonliterate.

These terms continue to subjugate and position multilingual students as inferior (see also Shannon, 1995) in classrooms. Politicians and ministries or departments of education point to low student test scores of rural multilingual students using monolingual assessments to determine learning. In contrast, scholars of multilingual students (García & Kleyn, 2016; Makalela, 2017) advocate for using students' linguistic and cultural resources as resources and skills in classrooms.

In her seminal book, *The Dreamkeepers: Successful Teachers of African American Children*, Ladson-Billings (1994) identified three features of successful teachers who worked with African American students in the context of US classrooms. Those components, which she collectively describes as 'culturally relevant pedagogy,' include teachers' focus on:

(a) *Student learning* and academic achievement, where learning is prioritized by teachers and they see their work as support their students' academic success by having high standards and expectations for students' learning.
(b) *Cultural competence*, in which teachers must possess knowledge of a minimum of two cultures, as bicultural educators. In this way,

teachers navigate cultural differences and do not see culture from a deficit perspective but rather a strength of students. Ladson-Billings (2017) describes that teachers can continue to acquire cultural competence in another culture and can strive to be multicultural. She advocates that teachers preferably have knowledge of more than two cultures.

(c) *Sociopolitical consciousness*, by which she refers to critical consciousness, or teachers' understanding of how society and politics position and further subjugate students from nonmainstream (non-white) backgrounds. Ladson-Billings (2017) argues that teaching is necessarily a political act.

Advocates of teaching and learning who recognize the social inequities that many of their students and families face and who seek to challenge and transform those inequities are referred to as *critical pedagogues*. They address implicit biases in education and society. Critical pedagogues view teaching as an inherently political act and they believe that knowledge is not neutral. Their work as teachers is interwoven with issues of social justice and they work toward an equitable school, community and world. In a recent discussion of her work, Ladson-Billings (2017) described how the socio-political component of culturally-relevant pedagogy, which is an integral part of the work of teachers of non-mainstream students, has been left aside or ignored.

Linguistically-Responsive Teacher Education

While Ladson-Billings addresses the cultural background of students, few educators have advocated for a framework of *linguistically*-relevant pedagogy. Some scholars and teacher-educators have extended the Culturally Relevant Pedagogy framework in the context of teacher preparation (Lucas, 2011; Lucas *et al.*, 2008), while others consider 'culturally and linguistically-relevant pedagogy' as conjoined in order to emphasize the relationship between culture and language (e.g. Hollie, 2017). Lucas and colleagues (2008) emphasize the need to prepare teachers and educators of diverse students to focus on language. They describe 'five essential understandings' that teachers of second language learners must have. Those understandings include knowledge that:

(1) Conversational language proficiency is fundamentally different from academic language proficiency, and academic language takes additional time (Cummins, 1981, 2000, 2008).
(2) Second language learners must have access to comprehensible input that is just beyond their current level of competence and opportunities to produce language (Krashen, 1982; Swain, 1995).
(3) Social interaction builds language development.

(4) Second language learners with strong native language skills are more likely to achieve parity with native-speakers over time (Cummins, 2000; Thomas & Collier, 2002).

(5) A safe, welcoming classroom environment with minimal anxiety about performing in a second language is essential (Krashen, 2003; Pappamihiel, 2002; Verplaetse & Migliacci, 2008).

(6) Some attention to linguistic form and function is essential to second language learning (Gass, 1997; Schleppegrell, 2004; Swain, 1995).

Lucas and colleagues' (2008) focus is on language as a transparent feature in teaching and learning for multilingual student. By transparent I mean that teacher-educators ensure that teachers know the role of language in schooling for rural multilingual students and how multilinguals can leverage this knowledge for further learning. Teachers can learn how text varies across various academic subjects and genres, and the differences between academic language and everyday conversation language. Making language 'visible' is similar to Cummins (2000) who describes how teachers and students must be 'language detectives'.

In 2011, Lucas refined her framework of linguistically responsive teacher education. They noted two key areas of teacher education essential to preparing linguistically responsive teachers: (a) teachers' *orientations* toward English (second) language learning students; and (b) teachers' knowledge and skills to effectively work with those students. Orientations include sociolinguistic consciousness or an awareness of the social uses and functions of language; and valuing linguistic diversity and maintaining a stance of advocacy for rural multilingual students. Knowledge and skills included four key areas: learning about students' backgrounds; identifying the language demands of the classroom; applying second language learning principles to the classroom; and scaffolding instruction for multilingual students' learning.

Tandon *et al.* (2017) examined Lucas's (2011) framework of linguistically responsive teaching. They researched the perceptions of 36 teacher candidates (TCs) or preservice teachers who were prepared to work with multilingual students who were English learners (ELs). Some of the candidates were novice beginning level teachers working with EL students in K-12 classrooms. They analyzed participants' essays and also interviewed them individually and in small focus groups. Tandon and colleagues found two key themes: first, the TCs demonstrated considerable anxiety regarding working with EL students, especially surrounding their ability to work and communicate with English learning students. They saw ELs as requiring significant additional work yet they felt largely unsure about what that might entail, such as scaffolding and teaching strategies. Second, the TCs needed additional preparation to demonstrate the range of linguistic responsiveness that is likely required in today's classrooms, particularly in the area of second language assessment.

Scholars have sought to identify what 'additional preparation' is needed for teachers of multilingual children. For instance, de Jong *et al.* (2013) described 'enhanced' knowledge and skills of teachers of multilingual students. Their research revealed three areas of knowledge and skills essential to teaching multilinguals. Those included a contextual understanding of students' linguistic and cultural experiences; knowledge and skills related to instruction for multilinguals; and expertise in navigating educational policies and practices for inclusive learning environments.

Research indicates that working with rural multilingual students is complex technical work that requires time, preparation and a deep understanding of students, families and the rural contexts in which education takes place (Knoche & Davis, 2017). It is easy to see how working with rural, multilingual families begins with who the students and families are and the sociopolitical context of education in a particular community. Returning to the work of Ladson-Billings as a lens for preparing teachers for multilingual students and families in rural settings, a framework of linguistically-responsive pedagogy would include these fundamental features:

(a) *Student learning* and academic achievement that *reflect the multiple languages that students use*, their ways of engagement in the world through those languages and the role that languages play in learning language and academic content. A focus on academic achievement of multilingual students means that languages are essential to students' educational experience, and each language is valued, fostered and used in accordance with students' multilingual repertoires. By multilingual repertoires I mean all of the knowledges and skills that a student possesses in order to engage in and interact with the world (García & Li Wei, 2014).

(b) *Linguistic competence* in which teachers of multilingual children have *knowledge of more than one language themselves*, in addition to knowledge of the developmental process of second language development and multilingualism. Teachers use their knowledge of languages and literacy development in order to facilitate their students' metalinguistic awareness. They may not know students' multiple languages, but they have a desire to learn how language shapes students' identities and their understanding of the world. Metalinguistic awareness refers to an individual's ability to view language as a process as well as an object. Developing metalinguistic awareness empowers multilingual students to make strategic language choices that reflect the context in which language use takes place.

(c) *Sociopolitical consciousness* in which teachers *understand and address the social and political positioning of languages in society*, multilingual students, and how languages are (de)valued in society by those who hold social, economic and political power. Teachers use their knowledge of languages in order to advocate for the development of multilingualism, multiple literacies and valid multilingual assessments for their students; and teachers' interactions with families occur in the languages that families speak and know in order to form trusting and caring relationships with them.

We will return to these three areas of linguistically-responsive pedagogy in the next chapter as a way to building awareness of multilingual families and advocating or acting with them.

Critical Consciousness: *Conscientização*

Like Ladson-Billings' work that seeks to challenge and transform the existing sociopolitical nature of education by addressing inequities in education, the work of educator Paulo Freire is situated in the sociopolitical context of students' lives. Freire is one of the most important critical pedagogues of the 20th century, and his theories continue to inform social justice and equity in education, as well as to advance a pedagogy of humanization.

Freire was born in northeast Brazil in 1921. He worked principally with rural and urban adults who were nonalphabet literate and who were socially, economically and politically oppressed by wealthy landowners and social class elites who took advantage of them. Farm workers were denied access to land, wealth and voting rights, which perpetuated their lower social class status. Freire witnessed how the cycle of oppression could be reconciled and challenged when 'illiterates' (his word) began to acquire literacy, specifically the ability to read and write, and to understand how adults' social position had been constructed for them. In other words, Freire understood how social inequities were the result of a contrived and 'constructed' social order, which he taught his students how to deconstruct and reconstruct in more equitable ways.

Over the course of his life's work, Freire developed very specific methods for teaching literacy to adults in urban and rural areas of Brazil that revolved around key ideas and terms that addressed the social inequities he saw. He used 'generative' words, or key words that people used to describe and convey their world. These were words that were important to the communities in which he worked. The words also had phonetic regularity (using a sound–symbol method of decoding words) and a potential to engage students in dialogue surrounding issues of oppression. Some examples of words he chose to use in Brazil with nonalphabet literate adults included: vote, brick, stove and people (Vittoria, 2014). Hence, the generative words were a foundation tool for building literacy (reading the word) and for addressing and transforming social inequities (reading the world).

Freire's work was not about teaching per se, as it was a philosophy of education and social change. He believed that the true goal of education was to liberate (hu)man through a process that he called *'conscientização.'* *Conscientização* is a process whereby people learn 'to perceive social, political, and economic contradictions, and to take action against the oppressive elements of reality' (Freire, 1997, loc. 512). To begin in the process of literacy learning and critical consciousness, Freire ruptured traditional teacher–student roles. He saw how the teacher-as-knower and student-as-learner dichotomy perpetuated social class differences. Thus, an essential feature of *conscientização* was the process of building relationships between two human beings. Freire characterized those relationships as 'loving, humble, hopeful, trusting, critical' (Freire & Macedo, 2001: 45).

Further reading of Freire's work elucidates these points; however, there are several key aspects to his work that are worth noting here. First, Freire believed that the key to a critical consciousness lay in dialogue between people and in relationship building. 'The correct method,' he wrote, 'lies in dialogue. The conviction of the oppressed that they must fight for their liberation is... a result of their own conscientização' (Freire & Macedo, 2001: 64).

Second, Freire refused to position people as minoritized as found in today's education literature, as terms such as minoritized reinforced notions of inferiority and limitation. In addition, Freire was vigilant that adults should be subjects-participants in the process of education rather than objects receiving education. Freire noted,

the oppressed are not 'marginals,' are not people living 'outside' society. They have always been 'inside'—inside the structure which made them 'beings for others.' The solution is not to 'integrate' them into the structure of oppression but to transform that structure so that they can become beings for themselves. (Freire & Macedo, 2001: 70)

Although the Brazilian context of education in the 1950s and 1960s may seem distant from today's fast-paced technological and global environment, Freire's pedagogy is central to an educators' work with and alongside multilingual families. His ideas remind us to reimagine relationships with rural multilingual students and families in personal dialogue. Specifically, Freirean pedagogy asks us to humanize our work by affirming the cultural and linguistic identities of our students and families, and to act so as to transform social spaces into places where equity and justice are the norm. Recall from earlier in this chapter that families seek to form relationships with educators. It is easy to see how knowledge of multilingual students and the pejorative ways that they are too often described and positioned socially intersects with Freire's message of transformation.

Finally, critical pedagogy, as educational theory and practice is grounded in social justice and equity, entails two steps are often referred to as 'praxis'. The term praxis is derived from the Greek word *praxis* (πρᾶξις). The term was associated with the idea of engaging in an activity, but it was later used to refer to action orientated work that leads to social change. The two steps of praxis include reflection and action, neither of which is easy or simple, despite the single word description. In the process of 'reflection' we continually reconsider social systems and privilege, and engage in theorizing about transforming schools for rural multilingual families through a lens of equity and justice. If we reflect without acting, then we are merely 'talking heads' or academics preaching from the ivory tower. On the other hand, if we act without careful reflection, we can act carelessly, lose focus of our work and feel overwhelmed in the injustices inherent in society. Freire posits that acting without reflection leads to either cynicism or total despair (1997). It is through these two steps that we will view rural multilingual family engagement in Chapter 3.

Relational Trust and Care

Rural multilingual families consistently describe one main theme in their relationship with educators – it is the theme of trust. Families' 'funds of knowledge' can only come into focus when trust is generated between educators and families. Building relationships and engaging in dialogue with multilingual families requires trust.

Byrk and Schneider (2002) describe relational trust as a main feature of school improvement. In their brief on relational trust, which involves relationships and trust between teachers, leaders and families, they describe relational trust as

> foster[ing] a set of organizational conditions, some structural and others social-psychological, that make it more conducive for individuals to initiate and sustain the kinds of activities necessary to affect productivity improvements. (Byrk & Schneider, 2002: 2)

Some of the key features of Bryk and Schneider's (2002) work as they relate to families include *respect* that is genuine listening and valuing the opinions of others; *personal regard for others*, which consists of being willing to extend oneself beyond what would normally be required; and *integrity*, or consistency between saying and doing. The authors' work has found some key conditions that foster relational trust. The importance of principal leadership, authentic parent engagement, small school size and stable (consistency in interactions) school communities. In sum, relational trust is adeptly aligned to rural schools in the sense that rural schools are frequently community sites and have strong educational leaders who understand how the community functions. Rural communities also have deep social networks where families rely on one another. Byrk and Schneider have found that schools that demonstrate a high degree of relational trust are more likely to raise student achievement than those with poor relationships. Relational trust building can be one purposeful goal of educators who work in rural schools with multilingual families.

Trust does not happen on its own or without sincere effort. Trust must be built and nurtured over time, repeated engagement with rural multilingual families, knowledge of who they are, where they are from and what they believe. For multilingual families, trust includes a sense of connecting with someone whom they can rely on to listen to their needs, understand what they are saying and why, and advocating for them when required. As the multilingual families noted above, lack of trust is one factor that impedes families from spending time in schools (Henderson & Mapp, 2002).

One way that educators build trust is by continually 'showing up', and being available and open to learning about rural multilingual students and families. Showing up is both literal and figurative. In other words, having a visible and physical presence in the community allows families to repeatedly see teachers and educators' commitment to their children. One teacher on our rural PD team noted that she attends weekend soccer (football) events where children from her school frequently play. Families see her present and gain a sense of belonging and building community when they see her. Figurative showing up means repeatedly acknowledging the cultural and linguistic strengths of families through a lens of care. It means ensuring, for example, that *every* school communication is written in culturally and linguistically appropriate ways for families, or that there are educators who can speak directly with families; that educators learn about their families' languages and use those languages – even in small ways – that demonstrate care; that there is an interpreter, cultural broker or guide available for families to help demystify how schools function and work; and that educators use their own 'cultural capital' (Bourdieu, 1986) to advocate for families, seeking dialogue and relationships with them.

Cummins *et al.* (2015) refer to the process of valuing and building upon students' linguistic and cultural knowledge as 'affirming identities'. Affirming identities of multilingual students has the benefits of supporting student learning and achievement; and of earning students' and families' trust and mutual care (Coady *et al.*, 2008). In other words, when educators affirm rural multilingual students' and families' identities, including their languages, cultures and literacies, they open the door to a humanizing relationship.

Trust and care go hand-in-hand. Care for another human being includes having a sense of empathy, critical consciousness and action. In fact, hooks (1994) describes how empathy in education emancipates teachers and school leaders from becoming scripted and listless in their work.

A short story demonstrates care and cross-cultural communication that builds relationships. A former student of mine graduated with her Master's degree in English to speakers of other languages (ESOL).

She was born in Puerto Rico and became a teacher of bilingual children for several years. She returned to school for her Master's degree. Upon completing her degree, Sara (not her real name) felt that it was important, in the midst of Islamaphobia and anti-Arabic sentiment in the USA, to move to Oman and to learn Arabic. She shared a story of her experience there. Sara wrote:

> During my last week in Oman, a group of 30 of us were exploring a small mountain village. We stumbled upon an old Omani lady who was so happy to see foreigners in her neck of the woods. She begged us to come inside for food and sweets and coffee. We explained that our group was massive and that despite her kindness there was no way she would be able to accommodate all of us and we would hate to impose. She responded, 'My house is small, but my heart is big.' And so this sweet lady fed all 30 of us strangers from the street and introduced us to her family.
>
> On the beach in Muscat I asked an Omani family if they could direct me to the nearest place to get food. Before we knew it, she had ordered food for us and her family brought it to the beach and we joined them for lunch, with no judgment of our lack of conservative clothing.
>
> May this language of love and hospitality be the one I become more fluent in than Arabic. This is what I want to bring home with me. In my country, sometimes we are so fast paced and concerned with making ends meet that we forget how to share and welcome every person we meet. Sometimes we forget what real wealth is. I hope that, of all the amazing things I learned abroad in Oman, this is the one I bring home.

This could be a story from a biblical or religious text, but it could also be a script from your rural classroom or a story from your home. Ultimately, this is a story that seeks to transcend differences across cultures, languages, politics and religion, and to transform difference into a humanizing pedagogy. Together, we are facing a new world, and we have a local and global imperative to reflect and act with rural multilingual families.

Conclusion

This chapter has provided a lens to frame our work with rural multilingual families. This chapter reviewed some of the contributions of critical pedagogues Ladson Billings and Freire. Their work provides a guide for transforming our work from a deficit view of multilingual families to one where families' languages and cultures bring resources to the school setting. Our critical lens was framed by linguistically-responsive pedagogy, a critical *conscientização* approach, and the need to build trust and demonstrate care for families. These provide a direction toward the goal of rehumanizing our relationships and engaging families. In addition, educators working with rural multilingual families might recognize how fostering relational trust with families can benefit schools and communities, and support student learning.

Activities

Activity 1

Personal educational history: Intergenerational trajectory

The purpose of this project is to encourage you to reflect upon how your personal educational experience is part of an intergenerational trajectory (Menard-Warwick, 2005) of education in your family. The notion here is that your perspectives on education are mediated by implicit and explicit messages you have received from your parents and/or caregivers and their experiences with schooling. These, in turn, are embedded within a broader social context. By reflecting upon your intergenerational educational trajectory you will be better able to appreciate that of your students.

Here are some questions to get you started:

- Where did you go to school?
- How did you feel about school?
- Did you see yourself as successful – why or why not?
- What made school easy for you compared to other students (e.g. parents were able to help you with homework, pay for private tutoring, Scholastic Aptitude Test (SAT) prep courses, etc.)?
- What made school difficult for you compared to other students?
- What effect did race, class, language, ethnicity, gender, ability have on your educational opportunities?
- What connections can you remember about your parents (grandparents, caregivers) and school?

Next, develop a set of questions that you might want to ask members of your family, including parents, grandparents, other caregivers and siblings (you might begin by asking the questions you asked yourself, above). Write your findings or share them in a small group. How does this activity relate to students you (will) teach?

Activity 2

Compare the two lists in this chapter: 'Challenges that educators say they face when working with multilingual families' and 'Challenges that rural multilingual families say they face.' With a colleague, read through the two lists out loud. How do educators' and families' voices sound? Feel? What themes do you notice? Identify one of the challenges from each list and talk-through a solution to those two challenges, using the framework of linguistically-relevant pedagogy and *conscientização*. How could you implement this solution in your school and community context?

References

Bourdieu, P. (1986) The forms of capital. In J. Richardson (ed.) *Handbook of Theory and Research for the Sociology of Education* (pp. 241–258). New York: Greenwood.

Byrk, A.S. and Schneider, B. (2002) *Trust in Schools: A Score Resource for Improvement.* New York: Russell Sage Foundation.

Coady, M. (2009) '*Solamente Libros Importantes*': Literacy practices and ideologies of migrant farmworking families in north central Florida. In G. Li (ed.) *Multicultural Families, Home Literacies and Mainstream Schooling* (pp. 113–128). Charlotte, NC: New Age.

Coady, M.R. and Yilmaz, T. (2017) Preparing teachers of ELs: Home-school partnerships. *TESOL Encyclopedia of English Language Teaching.* New York: Wiley.

Coady, M., Cruz-Davis, J. and Flores, C. (2008) *Personalmente*: Home-school communication practices with (im)migrant families in north Florida. Special Topics Issue, *Bilingual Research Journal* 31, 251–270.

Cochran-Smith, M., Barnatt, J., Lahann, R., Shakman, K. and Terrell, D. (2009) Teacher education for social justice: Critiquing the critiques. In W. Ayers, T. Quinn and D. Storall (eds) *Handbook of Social Justice in Education* (pp. 625–639). New York: Routledge.

Cummins, J. (1981) The role of primary language development in promoting educational success for language minority students. In *Schooling and Language Minority Students: A Theoretical Framework* (pp. 3–49). Sacramento, CA: California Department of Education.

Cummins, J. (2000) *Language, Power, and Pedagogy: Bilingual Children in the Crossfire.* Clevedon: Multilingual Matters.

Cummins, J. (2008) Teaching for transfer: Challenging the two solitudes assumption in bilingual education. In J. Cummins and N.H. Hornberger (eds) *Encyclopedia of Language and Education*: *Bilingual Education* (Vol. 5., 2nd edn, pp. 65–75). Boston, MA: Springer.

Cummins, J., Hu, S., Markus, P. and Kristina Montero, M. (2015) Identity texts and academic achievement: Connecting the dots in multilingual school contexts. *TESOL Quarterly* 49, 555–581. DOI: 10.1002/tesq.241

Dana, N. and Yendol-Hoppey, D. (2014) *The Reflective Educator's Guide to Classroom Research: Learning to Teach and Teaching to Learn through Practitioner Inquiry.* New York: Corwin.

de Jong, E.J., Harper, C.A. and Coady, M.R. (2013) Preparing mainstream teachers for CLD students: Enhancing the knowledge and skills that teachers of CLDs must have. *Theory into Practice Journal* 52 (2), 89–97.

Domínguez, M. (2017) 'Se hace puentes al andar': Decolonial teacher education as a needed bridge to culturally sustaining and revitalizing pedagogies. In D. Paris and H.S. Alim (eds) *Culturally Sustaining Pedagogies: Teaching and Learning for Justice in a Changing World* (pp. 225–246). New York: Teachers College Press.

Flores, N. and Rosa, J. (2015) Undoing appropriateness: Raciolinguistic ideologies and language diversity in education. *Harvard Educational Review* 85 (2), 149–171. DOI: 10.17763/0017-8055.85.2.149

Freire, P. (1997) *Pedagogy of the Oppressed.* New York: Bloomsbury.

Freire, A.M.A. and Macedo, D. (2001) *The Paulo Freire Reader.* New York: Continuum.

García, O. (2009) *Bilingual Education in the 21st Century: A Global Perspective.* Malden, MA: John Wiley.

García, O. and Kleyn, T. (eds) (2016) *Translanguaging with Multilingual Students: Learning from Classroom Moments.* New York: Routledge.

García, O. and Li Wei (2014) *Translanguaging: Language, Bilingualism and Education.* New York: Palgrave Macmillan.

Gass, S.M. (1997) *Input, Interaction, and the Second Language Learner.* Mahwah, NJ: Lawrence Erlbaum.

Henderson, A.T. and Mapp, K.L. (2002) *A New Wave of Evidence: The Impact of School, Family and Community Connections on Student Achievement.* Austin, TX: Southwest Educational Development Laboratory.

Hollie, S. (2017) Center for Culturally Responsive Teaching. See https://www.culturallyresponsive.org.

Hooks, B. (1994) *Teaching to Transgress: Education as the Practice of Freedom*. New York: Routledge.

Jeynes, W.H. (2003) A meta-analysis: The effects of parental involvement on minority children's academic achievement. *Education and Urban Society* 35 (2), 202–218.

Kisthardt, W.E. (2012) Integrating the core competencies in strengths-based, person-centered practice: Clarifying purpose and reflecting principles. In D. Saleebey (ed.) *The Strengths Perspective in Social Work Practice*. Upper Saddle River, NJ: Pearson.

Knoche, L.L. and Davis, D.L. (2017) Rural language and literacy connections: An integrated approach to supporting low-income preschool children's language and literacy development. In G.C. Nugent, G. M, Kunz, S.M. Sheridan, T.A. Glover and L.L. Knoche (eds) *Rural Education Research in the United States* (pp. 181–199). Switzerland: Springer International.

Krashen, S.D. (1982) *Principles and Practices in Second Language Acquisition*. New York: Pergamon Press.

Krashen, S.D. (2003) *Explorations in Language Acquisition and Use*. Portsmouth, NH: Heinemann.

Ladson-Billings, G. (1994) *The Dreamkeepers: Successful Teachers of African American Children*. San Francisco, CA: Jossey-Bass.

Ladson-Billings, G. (2017) *Culturally Responsive Pedagogy*. Keynote presentation at the National Teacher Leadership Conference. March 2–3, 2017. Miami, Florida.

Lucas, T. (2011) *Preparing Teachers for Linguistically Diverse Classrooms: A Resource for Teachers*. New York: Routledge/Taylor & Francis.

Lucas, T., Villegas, A.M. and Freedson-Gonzalez, M. (2008) Linguistically responsive teacher education: Preparing classroom teachers to teach English language learners. *Journal of Teacher Education* 59, 361–373. DOI: 10.1177/0022487108322110

Makalela, L. (2017) Language policy in Southern Africa. In T.L. McCarty and S. May (eds) *Encyclopedia of Language and Education, Vol. 1 Language Policy and Political Issues in Education* (3rd edn, pp. 519–529). Switzerland: Springer. New York: Springer.

Menard-Warwick, J. (2005) Intergenerational trajectories and socio-political context: Latina immigrants in adult ESL. *TESOL Quarterly* 39 (2), 165–185. DOI: 10.2307/3588307

Moll, L.C., Amanti, C., Neff, D. and Gonzalez, N. (1992) Funds of knowledge for teaching: Using a qualitative approach to connect homes and classrooms. *Theory Into Practice* 31, 132–141.

Pappamihiel, N.E. (2002) English as a second language students and English language anxiety: Issues in the mainstream classroom. *Research in the Teaching of English* 36, 327–355.

Ruiz, R. (1984) Orientations in language planning: Problem, right, or resource. *NABE Journal* 8 (2), 15–34.

Saleebey, D. (2012) *The Strengths Perspective in Social Work Practice*. Upper Saddle River, NJ: Pearson.

Schleppegrell, M. (2004) *The Language of Schooling: A Functional Linguistics Perspective*. Mahwah, NJ: Lawrence Erlbaum.

Shannon, S. (1995) The hegemony of English: A case study of one bilingual classroom as a site of resistance. *Linguistics and Education* 7, 175–200.

Swain, M. (1995) Three functions of output in second language learning. In G. Cook and B. Seidlehofer (eds) *Principle and Practice in Applied Linguistics: Studies in Honour of H. G. Widdowson* (pp. 125–144). Oxford: Oxford University Press.

Tandon, M., Viesca, K. M., Hueston, C. and Milbourn, T. (2017) Perceptions of linguistically responsive teaching in teacher candidates/novice teachers. *Bilingual Research Journal* 40 (2), 154–168. DOI: 10.1080/15235882.2017.1304464

Thomas, W.P. and Collier, V.P. (2002) *A National Study of School Effectiveness for Language Minority Students' Long-term Academic Achievement*. Santa Cruz, CA: University of California, Center for Research on Education, Diversity, and Excellence.

Verplaetse, L.S. and Migliacci, N. (2008) Making mainstream content comprehensible through sheltered instruction. In L.S. Verplaetse and N. Migliacci (eds) *Inclusive Pedagogy for English Language Learners: A Handbook of Research-informed Practices* (pp. 127–165). New York: Lawrence Erlbaum.

Vittoria, P. (2014) Dialogue in critical pedagogy: Generative word as counter-hegemonic action. *International Journal of Educational Policies* 8 (2), 103–114.

Weiss, H. (2014) Transatlantic forum on inclusive early years. 3rd Meeting. January 20–22, 2014. Lisbon, Portugal. See https://www.youtube.com/watch?v=Pv7VgChSg 8s&feature=share&list=PL17gcPJzCrQWAyCa5Lt5mOCKbDFTb4QN7.

Witte A. L. and Sheridan, S.M. (2011) *Family Engagement in Rural Schools*. R2Ed Working Paper No. 2011-2, National Center for Research on Rural Education. See https://r2ed.unl.edu/resources/downloads/2011-wp/2011_2_Witte_Sheridan.pdf.

3 Family-Centered Differentiated Engagement

Highlights

- Review of family engagement practices from a Western approach.
- Family-centered, differentiated engagement with multilingual families.
- Activities for further learning.

Real Scenario

It is Tuesday evening at 6 pm, and the school's Parent Leadership Council (PLC) meeting with rural multilingual families is about to begin. The goal of the one-hour, biannual meeting – a requirement by the federal government – is to inform parents about upcoming student tests and assessments; changes to the academic calendar, such as holidays and policies; and to ensure that parents know who the leadership of the school is when they have questions. Ultimately, the aim of these meetings is to foster families' engagement in their child's learning. Although only 12 families out of 40 replied to the bilingual (Spanish-English) paper invitation sent out the week before indicating that they would attend, only two families show up to the school with four children. Two of the students are older and attend secondary school. In the room are the school's guidance counselor, principal, bilingual paraprofessional who serves as the meeting interpreter, the district second language coordinator and several teachers – totalling about a dozen education professionals. The parents sit at round tables in the school media center and quietly eat pizza, which was ordered and paid for using school funds. The school staff proceeds to convey the information on the agenda to the parents, with the bilingual paraprofessional interpreting as the staff members speak. Parents listen quietly and nod their heads when asked if they understand the message of the meeting.

In the scenario above, what comes to your mind? I was present at the meeting and the scene was uncomfortable to watch. What did families really understand, what did they learn, and how did they perceive the goals of and outcomes from the meeting? In my experience with rural multilingual family engagement, the scenario above is quite typical. Despite the best intentions of the staff, the meeting was 'school-centered' and felt like a one-way process of communication (Warren *et al.*, 2009). School-centered meetings put the school's needs and messages at the forefront rather than truly understanding and listening to families, who they are and how they want to engage in education.

School leaders seeking rural multilingual family engagement need to reconceptualize their stance by shifting from a school-centered to family-centered approach, where families' languages, cultures and knowledges are the starting point for ongoing culturally and linguistically responsive engagement. Rural multilingual family-centered engagement, however, cannot be the same for all families. Rather, it must be differentiated based on who families are, what they know and need, and the resources that they bring to the school environment, including home languages, social networks, cultural practices in parenting, and beliefs and experiences about education.

Introduction

Family engagement in education has a long history and there have been key research studies on family engagement in schools for more than 40 years (Henderson & Mapp, 2002). Today, parents or caregivers are commonly referred to as a child's 'first teacher' and indeed healthy families are essential to child development and growth. Despite this notable body of research, there remain questions regarding how best to engage rural multilingual families in ways that optimize a child's learning. This is especially true when families speak different languages than those used in schools. In addition, how best to prepare teachers and educational leaders to foster and build relationships with rural multilingual remains largely undocumented in the research on education and family engagement.

This chapter examines several models of parent involvement and family engagement. This is not an exhaustive review of the literature, but rather a look at current practices on parental involvement or family engagement that are common in the literature on families and models of engagement.

Henderson and Mapp's Synthesis of Research

Two noteworthy scholars in the field of parental involvement are Henderson and Mapp (2002). In their extensive review of the research related to parental involvement, these scholars sought to understand and synthesize the research conducted on parental involvement. They followed a systematic, step-by-step approach to identifying empirical research studies conducted over that prior decade that would shed light on what we know to be best practices with parents and families. Henderson and Mapp's studies are indexed in their work, *A New Wave of Evidence* (2002). Of the 51 included studies, only a few were considered experimental or quasi-experimental research designs, in which participants were randomly assigned to a specific treatment, such as a school program or family engagement intervention in order to understand how those efforts affected student achievement. A larger number of Henderson and Mapp's research studies were correlational studies. In those studies, the researchers made associations or links between parental involvement and student learning outcomes. In addition, a significant number of the studies they reviewed were evaluations of programs or interventions, such as parent programs funded under the US Department of Education for high poverty schools (referred to as Title I), or smaller scale projects such as 'Book Buddies'.

Findings from their thorough review and analysis placed the studies in three main categories: those that investigated the *impact* of family and communities on student achievement; those that investigated *strategies* to connect schools, families and communities; and those that investigated *organizing efforts* to improve schools' engagement of parents and communities.

The authors identified three overarching features of high performing schools that engaged families. In those schools, successful educators:

• focused on building trust and relationships between teachers, families and key community organizations;
• identified, respected and acted upon families' needs, social class and cultural differences; and
• embraced a shared partnership of power and responsibility with families (Henderson & Mapp, 2002: 7).

Henderson and Mapp's review noted that schools where students are performing well have high levels of family and community involvement. They argue that the role of families cannot be underestimated: children whose parents talk with them about education, convey high expectations for their learning and plan for them to continue into college or university perform best overall. Some of the main associations that negatively affect student performance include poverty, parents having a lower level of education and a low level of literacy (ability to engage with text) in the homes. For multi (bi-)lingual families, issues of 'feeling welcome' (Henderson & Mapp, 2002: 159) and not feeling judged also affected their participation in schools and school events.

These findings echo those of Baquedano-López *et al.* (2013), who reviewed literature on parental involvement. They found that 'parental participation in schools is strongly shaped by [teachers'] perceptions of parents' background, the roles expected of them by school administrators and teachers, and by the organizations that fund... parental involvement programs' (Baquedano-López *et al.*, 2013: 150). In other words, the authors found that *what educators think* about and expect from parents has a strong impact on actual parental participation. Questioning our assumptions about multilingual families and reshaping our thinking as educators, then, from deficit and negative ideologies and stereotypes to actual knowing rural multilingual families is a first step toward building trust and care.

Epstein's Model of Spheres of Influence

Another important scholar in the field of parent involvement is Epstein (2011, whose work has identified a variety of school-based practices that support home–school–community partnerships. Epstein's work over the past 25 years has identified a broad array of hands-on strategies and activities for schools to use. Epstein's model consists of three overlapping spheres – home, school and community – and six types of involvement, which she refers to as 'six types of caring' (Epstein, 2011: 14). These are depicted in Figure 3.1.

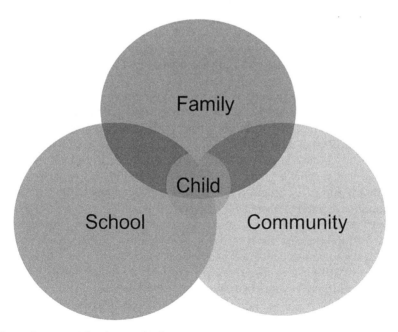

Figure 3.1 Epstein's spheres of influence
Source: Reproduced with permission from Epstein (2011)

ɔstein's classification of six types of involvement include the ꞈing:

- *Parenting* – helping all families to establish home environments to support children as students.
- *Communicating* – designing effective school-to-home and home-to-school communications about school programs and children's progress.
- *Volunteering* – recruiting and organizing parent help.
- *Learning at home* – providing information and ideas to families about how to help students at home with homework and other school tasks.
- *Decision making* – including parents in school decisions and leadership.
- *Community collaborating* – identifying and integrating resources and services from the community to support schools and families.

In her handbook on parental involvement, Epstein *et al.* (2008) offer multiple sample practices in each of the six areas of involvement. For example, communicating with parents includes activities such as setting up conferences with parents at least once each year. These are considered good educational practices that involve parents. In a more recent iteration of the work, Epstein describes 'redefinitions for parental involvement.' Epstein *et al.* (2011) acknowledge that communication should include multiple channels of communication that take into consideration parents who do not speak English or the main language of school. Epstein's model underscores the need for multiple levels of school leadership in order to build parent involvement in schools.

While these models tend to depict some best practices for engaging families, for rural multilingual families, the suggestions offered by Epstein and colleagues (2008) are static lists of activities that are unaligned to the realities of multilingual families today. These activities must be situated or contextualized for multilingual families; unpacked, decoded and described for families; and reconceptualized for multilingual families in rural settings. For example, conducting financial aid workshops for parents in the USA often assumes that parents have a high level of English language ability, deep knowledge of how higher education works and what it costs, awareness of immigration laws that affect students' participation and admission to college (and also financial aid) and parents' prior experiences in school or universities. Without a family-centered approach that first seeks to know families and understand their sociohistorical backgrounds, families are likely to feel overwhelmed and alienated. This is one reason why educators lament that multilingual families are 'absent' from school events and activities such as parent–teacher conferences and workshops on college applications.

Van Wyk and Lemmer (2009) applied Epstein's framework to parental involvement in education in South Africa. They describe South Africa as 'the Rainbow Nation' associating South Africa's diversity with the multiple colors of a rainbow and the rainbow itself signifying a single, unified phenomenon (Van Wyk & Lemmer, 2009: 164). Applying Epstein's Western framework and lens to South Africa, however, failed to illuminate the cultural beliefs, attitudes, assumptions and orientations toward parents, families and communities. Without understanding the sociohistorical and political context of education in South Africa, it is difficult, if impossible, to apply the framework to the realities of educators, children and families.

In addition, parenting is a culturally-informed activity. As noted earlier, among multilingual families, immigrant families and other 'nontraditional' families, parents themselves might not be the main caregivers of children. Moreover, they may have differing experiences and expectations about the role of parents in schools. For example, in our partner school district, some of the multilingual children were 'sent' to the USA by their biological parents in their home countries of China, Korea and Guatemala. A family friend considered to be an 'aunt' may, in fact, be the primary caregiver of the child. Sometimes family 'brothers' are biological cousins, but they are both growing up in the same household while one of the child's parents remains in the home country.

Parents or caregivers also hold experiences and diverse cultural beliefs regarding their roles in the education of children. Some will not feel comfortable facilitating homework with children, and many multilingual families feel that their knowledge of language or literacy development may be too limited to help their children learn to read and write at home (Coady & Moore, 2010). However, families can ensure that children have a quiet space to complete homework at night and have children describe their work to them.

While Epstein's model offers sample parent involvement events, such as activities for reaching out to families and providing communication strategies and models for community partnerships, these strategies perpetuate a one-size fits all, static and fossilized view of families that fail to affirm who multilingual families are and how they function. Rather, following an approach that examines the role of language, culture and context for multilingual families leads toward a differentiated family-centered approach.

Arias and Morillo-Campbell's Nontraditional Approach to Latino Parental Involvement

In their policy brief on working with English learners and parents, Arias and Morillo-Campbell (2008) describe the barriers that non-English speaking families face when attempting to integrate and communicate

with schools. Though this policy brief is not a model of family engagement, the authors offer several astute insights into the challenges and pos-
sibilities of effective family engagement. They note that the current
context of multilingual families in the USA is anti-immigrant and English-
only. These broader political policies make schools 'contested sites for the
acculturation of multilingual families' (Arias & Morillo-Campbell, 2008:
8). In other words, anti-immigrant policies devalue home cultures and
languages. Moreover, in 'anti-immigrant' climates, undocumented families will not risk leaving their homes other than for work, to grocery shop
or for emergency medical care. The anti-immigrant, anti-'other' political
climate has made schools and even churches contested sites, where families feel less safe.

The authors further describe challenges to traditional forms of parental involvement, due to parents' race, class, immigration status, level of
education or (English) language proficiency levels. The authors argue that
multilingual families feel marginalized at schools, yet their marginalized
status does not erode their desire to help their children in school. The
authors note schools' barriers, including: maintaining deficit views of parents; having a one-way approach to communication with parents; and
having an unwelcoming environment for parents.

In Table 3.1, Arias and Morillo-Campbell (2008) contrast traditional
and nontraditional approaches to parental involvement for families. Based
on their work, Arias and Morillo-Campbell suggest a 'non-traditional
model' of parent involvement (Arias & Morillo-Campbell, 2008: 11) that
departs from school-centered activities to a model that is based on a reciprocal understanding of schools, families and relationships. Schools and
educators build on the strengths of the family rather than consider them
to be deficits.

Table 3.1 Traditional versus nontraditional English learner parent involvement

Traditional	Nontraditional
Assist families with parenting and childrearing, create home conditions for learning	Develop reciprocal understanding of schools and families
Communicate with families about school programs and student progress	Situates cultural strengths of family and community in the school curriculum
Include recruiting efforts to involve families as volunteers/audiences	Promote parental advocacy that informs and teaches parents how to advocate for their children
Include families as participants in school decisions and governance	Instill parental empowerment through parent-initiated efforts at school and community
Collaborate with work and community-based agencies, colleges	Implement culturally and linguistically appropriate practices in all aspects of communication

Source: Adapted from Arias & Morillo-Campbell, 2008

As a starting point for multilingual families, the authors advocate the following actions: (a) support traditional parental involvement programs, but ensure that they are modified to be culturally and linguistically appropriate; (b) fund nontraditional parental involvement programs that reflect two-way 'reciprocal' understanding and communication practices; (c) support educators who can identify resources for curriculum and school outreach; and (d) support community-based education programs to inform parents of cultural differences, values and expectations of schools. The emphasis on the cultural and linguistic backgrounds of families and the addition of home culture and language embedded in the school curriculum are essential to moving beyond 'inclusion' or 'involvement' to integrating multilingual families into schools.

WIDA's A, B and Cs of Parent Engagement

The WIDA group (WIDA, 2017) is a team of professional educators and scholars who focus on second language development, instruction and assessment based in the USA, but also extend worldwide. One component of their work includes family engagement that is linguistically and culturally responsive to multilingual families and children. They note that family engagement consists of building a relationship between families that is ongoing, mutual, built on trust and respect, and that focuses on student learning and achievement.

The WIDA group has designed an approach to prepare educators for multilingual family engagement that they refer to as the ABCs. Because there is no one-size-fits all approach to family engagement, they offer this framework to outline six essential areas in three categories (A, B and C) that educators can be aware of when working with multilingual families:

- A – Awareness and advocacy.
- B – Brokering and building trust.
- C – Communication and connect to learning.

The WIDA team notes that working with families requires the first step of becoming aware of who families are, building trust and communicating with them. Becoming aware involves educators' taking stock of their personal views of working with families and their beliefs about how parents should be involved in a child's education. Similar to Henderson and Mapp's (2002) review of research that educators' views and beliefs had a strong impact on parental involvement in schools, WIDA suggests that advocacy is a 'tool that parents and educators can use to fight injustices' (WIDA, 2017: 2).

Brokers are cultural informants or people with language skills and knowledge of the community who can serve as mediators between schools and families. The WIDA team notes that this can include cultural brokers as well as linguistic brokers. Multilingual children should not serve as cultural brokers or interpreters on behalf of parents or caregivers, because it places undue stress and responsibility on children (Orellana, 2009). Ensuring two-way communication with multilingual families in languages that that they use is one way to build trust with them. Moving from school-centered to family-centered engagement means that communication should flow from school to home to school to home in a continuous recursive manner, where schools consistently respond to the needs and requests of families and also initiate and follow through in communication. Finally, the WIDA group suggests that connecting parents to their child's learning should be focused and systemic, and requires that families are given information that is timely and understandable.

A Model for Educators: Differentiating Family Engagement for Rural Multilingual Families

It is easy to see the commonality among scholars reviewed above and their contributions to family engagement. Scholars would largely agree that engaging families is a worthwhile activity and an essential component to supporting student success, including academic achievement and social emotional well-being. High performing schools, that is, schools where students are doing well and achieving academically, also appear to have engaged parents (Bryk & Schneider, 2002; Goodall & Montgomery, 2014), yet there is a need to move from school-centered to family-centered approaches to engagement, and taking an inventory of family strengths by conducting an assessment of the school and context. Learning about rural multilingual families' home cultures, languages, literacies, and needs is the first step. As Arias and Morillo-Campbell (2008) note, multilingual families differ tremendously in their configuration; definitions of family; their home languages and literacy practices; access to resources such as food, transportation and work; beliefs about education; and experiences with education themselves. That knowledge must be starting points for educators.

Figure 3.2 is a circular model that shows how engagement with multilingual families can be more broadly conceptualized to build relationships with families; learn about the sociohistorical, political, and languaging experiences of families; and situate that knowledge in local communities. It also shows that family engagement is a continuous process and addresses the realities of multilingual families in rural settings.

One of the first steps of educators is to learn about their multilingual families, their home languages and literacy practices, cultures and needs. Educators can learn about families through their students, by making appointments for home visits, learning about immigrant families' home countries and taking stock of local industries, labor, commerce and agencies. They can also learn about family and local migration patterns and the history of the community and local political that build a positive 'context of reception' for immigrants (Stepick & Dutton Stepick, 2009).

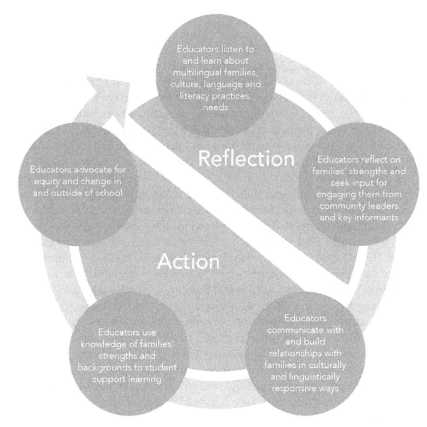

Figure 3.2 Differentiated family engagement for educators
Source: Maria Coady/Lianne Jepson Guerra

For example, in our work, we conducted an inventory of local community resources such as public libraries, health and dental clinics, and social service agencies. We then worked with our community partner to created and translate a bilingual resource guide for families that was printed (due to limited internet availability) and that had simplified text, making the guide easy to read. We worked with our partners to show rural multilingual families how to use the guide, modeling how to identify services and which had multilingual staff.

Continuing along the model, educators reflect on the needs of rural multilingual families, including their access to food and addressing food insecurity over the weekends when school meals are not available; reliable transportation and the cost of transportation to and from school, community centers and medical care; and knowledge of how the community functions. For example, how do families contribute to the local community? The local economy? What strengths do families bring, including their linguistic and culturally diverse ways of being and knowing the world? School leaders and educators can identify key community members or leaders who can act as 'cultural informants' to the school.

In a school in northern Alabama where immigrant families were working in chicken processing plants, families trusted and relied on one key bilingual community member or cultural 'informant' to act as a liaison with the school. The school leaders communicated key events to the families via the informant. Together, they designed and arranged for annual school events, such as the 'decorate the school' weekend in May. On that weekend, families came to school each year to paint walls and depict local, cultural iconography that represented the families' rich traditions and cultural backgrounds.

These practices inform the next area of the framework, which is communicating with families in their home languages, building and earning trust, and demonstrating care of families and children. Communication with rural multilingual families is consistent and involves identifying spaces in the rural community convenient for families and where families feel safe to attend. Rural locales may only have a school site that serves as a community center. In other places, community centers may be more friendly, welcoming and nurturing spaces for multilingual families than schools (Coady *et al.*, 2015; Marquardt *et al.*, 2011). This phase underscores an ongoing, regular and systematic approach to communicating with families in languages that they know. Educators learn the languages that families use and understand the pragmatics features of a language such as social distance between speakers that are invisible features of communication. Ongoing reflection and assessment of this aspect is essential, because families in rural settings may be mobile and move frequently in and out of the community. Updating communication methods, phone numbers and contact information is the work of educators in order to remain connected to rural multilingual families. For nonliterate families, access to interpreters and community members who speak their families' languages can be kept near families' information.

Differentiated engagement with rural multilingual families next involves educators who use their knowledge of the sociohistorical and political context of families, situated and rooted in the local community, to make informed instructional decisions that support student learning. Families contribute to the overall social environment of the local community, the economy and the way that the community functions.

Finally, educators recognize the local and global contexts in which rural multilingual families live and in which schools function. In 'contested' spaces, engaging with families means that educators are open to listening to and responding to families' needs. This is where advocacy for families occurs. For example, access to dental care and services is not only expensive in the USA, but in rural settings, identifying pediatric dentists who speak the languages of multilingual families is challenging. Over the years, we have identified local dentists who will work gratis or on a sliding scale for immigrant families who have no access to health insurance. We have driven families to low-income dental clinics and identified financial support to families in need of dental care. Each family's need was different and each family's situation warranted a differentiated response to advocating for the children both in and outside of school. Advocating means being willing to listen to families and help to identify solutions that support children's learning and overall well-being.

This model of differentiated family engagement entails both reflection and action. Listening, learning and reflecting on family strengths and needs encompass the first part of the model. Acting with rural multilingual families involves communicating, using information to support student learning and advocating for a socially just society. These two areas – reflection and action – are described further in Chapters 4 and 5.

Conclusion

This chapter reviewed some Western models and approaches to parental involvement. These all offered examples of effective ways to engage families. However, there is no one-size-fits all approach and rural multilingual families require nontraditional, creative approaches to engagement. I offered a model for 'differentiated family engagement'. In the following chapter, I describe a two-step process and specific strategies for differentiating rural multilingual family engagement, beginning with educators' personal educational history and conducting an informal assessment of rural multilingual families strengths and resources.

Activity

Activity 1

Compare the four approaches to parental involvement in this chapter: Henderson and Mapp, Epstein, Arias and Morillo-Campbell, and the WIDA group's ABCs. What are some of the commonalities across these three sets of authors' work with families? What are some ways that they

	Henderson & Mapp	Epstein	Arias & Morillo-Campbell	WIDA ABCs
	Three overarching features of high performing schools	Three spheres and six types of parental involvement	Traditional versus nontraditional EL parental involvement	Six essential areas: As, Bs, Cs
Features of these approaches				
How rurality affects these approaches?				
How multilingualism affects these approaches?				

differ? Finally, how will addressing the nature of 'rurality' and multilingualism affect these different approaches?

References

Arias, M.B. and Morillo-Campbell, M. (2008) Promoting ELL parental involvement: Challenges in contested times. Boulder, CO: Education Policy Research Unit. ERIC Document ED506652. See https://eric.ed.gov/?id=ED506652

Baquedano-López, P., Alexander, R.A. and Hernandez, S.J. (2013) Equity issues in parental and community involvement in schools: What teacher educators need to know. *Review of Research in Education* 37, 149–182.

Bryk, A.S. and Schneider, B. (2002) *Trust in Schools: A Score Resource for Improvement.* New York: Russell Sage Foundation.

Coady, M. and Moore, C. (2010) Using *Libros*: The emergent bi-literacy development of Spanish-speaking children. *TESOL Journal* 2, 91–108.

Coady, M.R., Coady, T.J. and Nelson, A. (2015) Assessing the needs of immigrant, Latino families and teachers in rural settings: Building home-school partnerships. *NABE Journal of Research and Practice* (6). See https://www2.nau.edu/nabej-p/ojs/index.php/njrp/article/view/42

Edwards, P.A. (2016) *New Ways to Engage Parents: Strategies and Tools for Teachers and Leaders, K-12.* New York: Teachers College Press.

Epstein, J.L. (2011) *School, Family, and Community Partnerships: Preparing Educators and Improving Schools* (2nd edn) Philadelphia, PA: Westview Press.

Epstein, J.L., Sanders, M.G., Sheldon, S., Simon, B.S., Salinas, K.C., Jansorn, N.R., VanVoorhis, F.L., Martin, C.S., Thomas, B.G., Greenfield, M.D., Hutchins, D.J., and Williams, K.J. (2008) *School Family, and Community Partnerships: Your Handbook for Action* (3rd edn). New York: Corwin.

Goodall, J. and Montgomery, C. (2014) Parental involvement to parental engagement: A continuum. *Educational Review* 66 (4), 399–410.

Grant, K.B. and Ray, J.A. (2015) *Home, School, and Community Collaboration: Culturally Responsive Family Engagement* (3rd edn) SAGE.

Henderson, A.T. and Mapp, K.L. (2002) *A New Wave of Evidence: The Impact of School, Family and Community Connections on Student Achievement.* Austin, TX: Southwest Educational Development Laboratory. See www.sedl.org/connections/resources/evidence.pdf.

Marquardt, M.F., Steigenga, T.J., Williams, P.J. and Vasquez, M.A. (2011) *Living "Illegal": The Human Face of Unauthorized Immigration.* New York: The New Press.

Orellana, M.F. (2009) Translating childhoods: *Immigrant youth, language, and culture.* New Brunswick, NJ: Rutgers University Press.

Stepick, A. and Dutton Stepick, C. (2009) Contexts of reception and feelings of belonging. *Forum: Qualitative Social Research* 10 (3), Art 15. See http://www.qualitative-research.net/index.php/fqs/article/view/1366/2863.

Van Wyk, N. and Lemmer, E. (2009) Organising parent involvement in SA schools. Cape Town: Juta.

Warren, M.R., Hong, S., Rubin, C.L. and Uy, P.S. (2009) Beyond the bake sale: A community based relational approach to parent engagement in schools. *Teachers College Record* 111, 2209–2254.

WIDA (2017) The A, B, Cs of family engagement. See https://wida.wisc.edu/resources/abcs-family-engagement

4 Praxis and Practice: Becoming *Aware* of Multilingual Families in Rural Settings

Highlights

- Connecting personal family histories and background to ideas of education.
- Strategies for learning about families.
- Identifying needs and challenges that families may face in rural communities.
- Activities for further learning.

Real Scenario

Suzanne is a guidance counselor at a grade 3–5 elementary school in a rural school district in north Florida. The local community economy relies on crop industries such as watermelon, peanuts and palm trees to support workers in the area. Many of the workers are from Central America who send their children to her school. For several years, Suzanne has been concerned about the limited communication she has had with rural multilingual parents who immigrated to the USA. She knows that the parents work long hours and that their primary language is Spanish, and although she has heard other languages spoken, she does not know what they are. She also knows that the children's parents travel significant distances to access resources such as food in the rural area. There is no public transportation system available in the community, so transportation is a major barrier to parents' physical presence in school. Beyond that, she does not know much about her students' families. Suzanne feels uncomfortable when she overhears staff state that the parents 'have no literacy' or that 'they don't care about their children's education' because they do not attend parent–teacher night at the school.

Introduction

Suzanne's dilemma is not unique among educational staff and teachers who seek to build relationships with rural multilingual families, but who do not see them physically present in schools. This chapter focuses on ways that educators can identify who their multilingual families are, their beliefs, cultures and home practices, and some tools that they can use to become better informed about families. I re-emphasize that communication is incumbent upon school educators and teachers to not only *initiate* communication, invitations and requests for information, but also to *sustain* communication by following up, taking action, demonstrating care and building trust. In other words, I am advocating a *school–home–school* (Olivos *et al.*, 2011) pattern of communication that ensures that the educational and social-emotional needs of children and families are a priority, not ignored, and that families and children do not 'fall through the cracks' of miscommunication.

This chapter underscores the first of a two-step process to build rural multilingual family engagement. It is insufficient for educators to know about the families' needs, cultures and languages, but not to act upon them in ways that affirm students' identities (ontology) and families' ways of knowing (epistemology) and participating in the world. Similarly, it is insufficient for educators to act or engage with families without understanding and becoming aware of who they are, how they function and what their needs are. In the latter case, action without reflection and knowledge can be misguided and culturally or linguistically inappropriate.

Definition cutout

Ontology refers to the nature of being, and one's identit(ies) in the world; 'to be'.
Epistemology refers to one's way of acquiring knowledge and the process of knowing and participating in the world; 'to know'.

Makalela (2015), who works in rural multilingual settings in South Africa, describes how in order for multilingual students to succeed academically, educators must first ensure that students' and families' identities are affirmed and reflected in school curricula, activities and events. In addition, students' and families' ways of knowing and participating in the world must likewise be reflected in the ways that schools function. This chapter addresses ways in which to become aware of families who use minoritized languages and whose cultural backgrounds and knowledge might differ from those of the school. Tables 4.2 and 4.3 (pp. 76–77) are guides to embark on promoting rural multilingual family engagement. Table 4.2 is a guide to learning about families' backgrounds, and Table 4.3 assists in connecting family background to student learning in the classroom.

Building Background

To begin learning about your school's multilingual families and students, it is first important to reflect on your own assumptions, beliefs and perceptions about education in general, the role of multiple languages and literacies in schools, and views and assumptions about multilingual families. You may have some strongly held beliefs about families or perhaps have too little information about families in your school community. Continuous self-reflection is essential to the art of education, because our beliefs and views change over time and what we once thought to be 'true' may later not be.

Zentella (2005: 21) notes that there are three main concerns with working with families in the context of multilingual settings, referring to them as possible 'pitfalls'. These are: (1) 'essentializing' families whereby we associate certain behaviors or ideologies as the essential characteristics of a group. This is especially problematic when considering issues of rurality, race, class, national origin, and language. (2) 'Privileging' one form of literacy, or for that matter, parenting behaviors over another. An example is the belief that all families read (or should read) bedtime stories to their children at night is something that elementary level teachers encourage in many homes. The idea of bedtime stories privileges white mainstream literacy activities over nontraditional mainstream literacies. And (3) following an 'implied determinancy' approach to family engagement, such as setting a prescriptive set of actions such as parents volunteering in the school and believing that those that will lead to specific outcomes, such as improved student achievement on a standardized test.

This last area, implied determinancy, is important because following a prescriptive set of actions reinforces stereotypes about families and students, and educational practices need to affirm new definitions and configurations of families (Edgell & Docka, 2007). Further, implied determinancy could further undermine personal relationship building that is necessary to foster trust and care between rural multilingual families and educators. For example, one misconception that educators hold of multilingual families is that the children should only read and speak the language of schooling in the home. This actually works against multilingual students and undermines first and second language development, yet educators believe that following X behavior will lead to Y outcome for all children.

For these three reasons – essentializing, privileging and implying determinancy – we begin this chapter with exploring your personal educational history, an activity introduced at the end of Chapter 2. If you have not completed that activity, reflect on your background and knowledge of your own educational history. You might ask yourself the following reflective questions:

• What was the role of home languages and literacy practices in my own educational experiences? For example, how did my family use various languages, if at all?

- What dialects were reflected in my own school experiences or home? Was the local dialect deemed to sound 'inferior' to a more standard form of language?
- What terminologies were used to describe people? Were they affirming or pejorative?
- What home literacy practices and traditional cultural practices did my family follow?

For example, did your family regularly engage in reading activities, sharing family histories orally or engage in certain religious practices? Were there educational expectations that differed for boys and girls? Make a list of those activities. Next, think about how those activities either supported and affirmed mainstream language and literacy practices or differed from those? What role did your family play in affirming school practices or differed from those? You can use imagery, words, sights and sounds to invoke your own personal reflection.

Christiansen (1998) designed a reflection activity that can be used on your own students as well as with colleagues in professional learning communities (PLCs). The goal of the following 'Where I'm From' poetry activity is to describe the diverse histories that each of us brings to the school community. Start by reading the poem by George Ella Lyon (1993) titled 'Where I'm From.' Note the physical object, sense of history, tradition, and culture that is evoked in the poem.

Where I'm From
George Ella Lyon
I am from clothespins,
from Clorox and carbon-tetrachloride.
I am from the dirt under the back
porch.
(Black, glistening
it tastes like beets.)
I am from the forsythia bush,
the Dutch elm
whose long gone limbs I remember
as if they were my own.
I am from fudge and eyeglasses,
from Imogene and Alafair.
I'm from the know-it-alls
and the pass-it-ons,
from perk up and pipe down.
I'm from He restoreth my soul
with a cottonball lamb
and ten verses I can say myself.
I'm from Artemus and Billie's
Branch,
fried corn and strong coffee.

From the finger my grandfather lost
to the auger
the eye my father shut to keep his
sight.
Under my bed was a dress box
spilling old pictures,
a sift of lost faces
to drift beneath my dreams.
I am from those moments –
snapped before I budded –
leaf-fall from the family tree.

After reading the poem, use a title such as 'I am from...' as a poem frame or poem starter to write a list of items, traditions, places, and events that characterize your background. Using multiple languages to convey the rich linguistic background of students is useful, and write words that 'sound like home' (Lyon, 1993: 3).

Share your organizer with colleagues (for educators) or peers (for students). Allow some time to write the words into a format similar to George Lyon's, or deviate and write a narrative using the same imagery and ideas. Share the poems out loud, taking care not to critique others' background but rather to seek additional information.

What insight did you glean about your family and its way of being in the world? What did you learn about your colleagues'? What might you learn about another family's way of being (ontology) and knowing (epistemology) of the world.

Learning about Families

The insight gained from the previous activity can be useful in exploring the literacies and languages of rural multilingual families in rural communities. To reiterate, you may hold assumptions about multilingual families, and it's important to examine those. What are some ways that you can obtain insight and information into families? Table 4.1 is a matrix that you could use to guide your investigation of multilingual family languages, literacies and cultural practices that influence how to they function, know and are. You might not obtain all of the information, but remember that this is a guide for you to use, adapt and modify as you see meets the background of the school and local community.

Table 4.1 Graphic organizer for 'I am from...'

I am from...	(sights, imagery, and landscapes)
I am from...	(objects and materials)
I am from...	(sounds)
I am from...	(family events or traditions)
I am from...	(family names and bilingual/multilingual words or phrases)

Table 4.2 My school's rural multilingual families

Family's background
Political and historical background
Geographic characteristics
Cultural characteristics (values, communication styles, gender roles, greetings)
Family's languages
Language(s) spoken or written in the home
Language abilities in the language of school (spoken or written)
Parent or caregiver desire to learn additional languages
Family's experiences
Reception by mainstream culture (acceptance or rejection), including immigration
Reasons for migrating (if applicable)
Degree to which families maintain cultural identities
Beliefs about education
Knowledge of schools and how they function
Local resources
Economic context
Social networking
Social services, including access to medical, dental and vision care
Labor and other work
Transportation

There are four key areas to investigate in rural settings: families' backgrounds, families' languages, families' experiences and local resources. These areas are reflected in Table 4.2. You may identify different areas to explore with colleagues or your school staff. The more you learn about your students' backgrounds and families histories, the more likely you are to design a family-centered approach to engaging multilingual families.

The next step is to connect this information to an action plan. Connect these questions about rural multilingual families to ways to find out and investigate who families are, what they believe, their linguistic and cultural strengths, and what they know about education. Some of the information in the column is intuitive and you will likely have access to information about rural multilingual families already. The final step is to connect that information to how this connects to student learning.

Recall that linguistically responsive pedagogy has a focus on linguistic competence, the sociopolitical context of education and student achievement. Rural multilingual families will want to know how they can support their children's education. Teachers of multilingual students have the ability to strategically connect students' background to learning (Coady *et al.*, 2016) when prepared to do so. See Table 4.3. These three areas – 'what I need to know', 'how I can learn about this' and 'how this connects

Table 4.3 Exploring family engagement for my students

What I need to know	How I can learn about this	How this connects to student learning
Sociopolitical context/background		
Home countries		
Cultural background (values, communication styles, gender roles, greetings)		
Language(s) spoken or written in the home		
Language abilities in English or language of school (spoken or written)		
Parent or caregiver desire to learn additional languages Beliefs about multilingualism and multiliteracies		
Reception by mainstream culture (acceptance or rejection), including immigration		
Reasons for migrating		
Degree to which family maintains cultural identities		
Beliefs about education		
Knowledge of schools and how they function		
Economic		
Social networking		
Social services, including access to medical, dental and vision care		
Labor and other work		
Transportation		

to student learning' – aim to build connections between students and learning. Using Tables 4.2 and 4.3 in our rural multilingual schools in teacher professional development, I have found that making these connections is not intuitive, even when teachers are prepared to do so (Coady *et al.*, 2016).

Table 4.4 is an example of a completed table with a multilingual family in a rural school district. While this is a large table of information, it clearly helps me as an educator to see the importance of knowing the community, its resources and some of the potential barriers to communication with multilingual families. One example is the assumptions about families' knowledge of how schools work and the roles of various educational staff and personnel. Recall earlier that what educators believe about families influences the rural multilingual engagement and that affects student learning. In some cultures, for example, the concepts of 'special education' programs or schools 'guidance counselors' are not shared educational practices. Special education services differ greatly around the world (Gargiulo & Bouck, 2017), and the USA has an extensive history of providing special education services, identification of services and assessment

Table 4.4 Example of a completed table for educators' family engagement

What I need to know	How I can learn about this	How this connects to student learning
Sociopolitical context	Research online about the region they are from, books and news events	Curriculum selection, narrative, text, discussion, build background
Geographic characteristics	Maps, materials online	Cultural knowledge, build background
Cultural background (values, communication styles, gender roles, greetings)	Online and print books on the culture, and videos from the region Ask children and family, ask local experts	Build background, connect students' knowledge to new knowledge
Language(s) spoken or written in the home	Online and print books on the culture, and videos from the region Ask children and family, ask local experts	Use of home language(s) for learning content and for supporting (second/English) language
Abilities in school language (written or spoken)	Ask children and family, ask local experts	Identify where students need support in listening, speaking, reading, writing
Parent or caregiver desire to learn additional languages Beliefs about multilingualism and multiliteracies	Ask family, ask local experts	Identify programs that support caregiver language development Reinforce use of multiple languages in the home
Reception by mainstream culture (acceptance or rejection), including immigration	Listening for views, assumptions, stereotypes and checking personal assumptions and beliefs	Provide space to challenge negative views and beliefs, support home culture and background, inform colleagues
Reasons for migrating (if applicable)	Ask children and family, ask local experts	Provide resources to children and families
Degree to which families maintain cultural identities	Ask family, ask cultural experts	Support home culture and make ongoing connections between home–school
Beliefs about education	Ask family	Inform, reinforce positive view of education and outcomes associated with education
Knowledge of schools and how they function	Ask family, check personal assumptions and beliefs	Provide families with knowledge about how schools work to build trust, communication and resources
Economic	Ask local experts, check online and print directories of the community	Identify resources where needed, including food safety, health
Social networking	Ask local experts and families	Mitigate isolation
Social services, including access to medical, dental, and vision care	Ask local experts and families	Provide school resources – food, school supplies, learning supports where available

(Continued)

Table 4.4 *(Continued)*

What I need to know	How I can learn about this	How this connects to student learning
Labor and other work	Ask local experts and families	Schedule communication with families during nonwork hours
Transportation	Ask local experts, check online and print directories of the community	Ensure that families can attend school events, children have safe transport to events

practices. Families from different countries may have little knowledge of these services and culturally some families may not recognize learning disabilities as such (Fadiman, 1998). What families know and believe about those disabilities and services influence the way that educators need to describe and discuss that information with them.

Recall the Álvarez family from the *Altiplano* region of Mexico. The family lived in a rural community where transportation was limited. As undocumented parents in a foreign country, they lived in fear that they would be caught driving with invalid drivers' licenses. While they waited for their legal paperwork to be processed – a process that took nearly 10 years – they remained close to home and accessed no social services for them. They were, essentially, socially and geographically isolated, but their social network extended into a nearby county where church services were held in Spanish.

I got to know the family over a period of about three years and I continue to see them at community events. Yet many educators at the children's schools did not know the parents, despite the family's atten-dance at key information events at the school, and what they did know that this was a low-income family with parents who 'spoke no English'. What assumptions did educators make about the family and their home language and literacy resources? What information might have sup-ported family engagement and actual relationship building in the school context? How could that information be used by teachers and school leaders?

While it is not possible to learn everything about the family, there are many things that we can learn and understand to identify ways to build relationships with the family and to support school–home–school com-munication. Table 4.5 is a completed table that represents what I learned about the Álvarez family.

Among rural multilingual families and schools, one of the areas of need is access to local services, something that families described in Chapter 2. As reflected in Tables 4.2 and 4.3, some of those services include transportation; medical, dental and vision care; food and medici-nal items; and social support networks from churches, libraries and com-munity centers, if those are available. In rural settings, social support

Table 4.5 The Álvarez family from Mexico

Family's background	
Political and historical background	Mexico has a rich history of indigenous communities and indigenous languages spoken. The political situation is currently stable, but local news suggests political unrest and the economic context is difficult.
Geographic characteristics	Rural community that is mountainous making travel difficult
Cultural characteristics (values, communication styles, gender roles, greetings)	Long history of working with fabric, *mantelas*. Girls fill traditional roles of cooking, cleaning and household chores. Both boys and girls attend school. However, secondary school can be distant and expensive for families
Family's languages	
Language(s) spoken or written in the home	Spanish is the language of parents' education. Otomí is spoken in the home as the oral language of communication, alongside Spanish and some English among the children.
Language abilities in English or language of school (spoken or written)	Children's literacy is English. There is some knowledge of written Spanish from church services
Parent or caregiver desire to learn additional languages	Parents would like to learn more English. The father uses English in the workplace, but the mother has less interaction through English in the community.
Family's experiences	
Reception by mainstream culture (acceptance or rejection), including immigration	Family is rural and access few or no services. They are largely isolated. It is unclear about the community reception, as few people locally speak Spanish and seem to know little about the *altiplano* region of Mexico.
Reasons for migrating (if applicable)	Economic opportunity for the parents and social mobility for the children.
Degree to which families maintain cultural identities	Strong sense of tradition and culture in the home. Local ingredients are used to prepare traditional foods. Traditional culture is important to the parents.
Beliefs about education	Parents want to support the children's learning. However, they believe that only school texts are important to read. They believe that educators/teachers are responsible for children's literacy development and learning.
Knowledge of schools and how they function	Know very little about services and school functioning. They have children translate school documents and trust their translation. Children also interpret for the parents at local events and in school meetings.
Local resources	
Economic	The family seems to struggle to make ends' meet. A fieldtrip that the daughter took was paid for by the mother selling tamales to her friends in local venues (at a plant nursery, at church).
Social networking	Some networking occurs in the church network and community about 60 miles away.
Social services, including access to medical, dental, and vision care	There is a local dental clinic but it is about 25 miles away. The local medical center is in a suburban setting about 10 miles away. The family has no medical insurance.
Labor and other work	There is no local transportation available. The father works on the home-site situated on a local farm.
Transportation	Father has access to a truck. Mother can drive but prefers not to. Neither parent will drive during heavy traffic times; fear of being pulled over.

networks build community, affirm families, and help to address some of the rurality and rural lifestyle that isolates families.

Media

In our local setting, immigrant, non-white and minoritized families and children contribute in many ways to the diversity of the community and to the way it functions. However, family contributions conflict with images that are portrayed on television, online and in social media, where rural multilingual families are stereotyped or invisible, as well as other forms of media, such as in school textbooks, in the literacy materials that students read, on the radio, in social media and so on.

Celebrating students' heritage is a common activity across US schools, such as Hispanic heritage month in September through October each year. However, celebrating a single month of any cultural group overlooks histories, contributions, languages and cultures that contribute to a multicultural community. In other words, multicultural, multilingual education should be integrated and interwoven into school curricula every day as a true reflection of the USA and of an inclusive educational curriculum (Sleeter, 2011).

After reflecting upon your personal educational or family history, and conducting some research about the multilingual families in your community, a next step is building an awareness of rural multilingual families, local resources and social networks. In our US context, immigrant families in rural settings are out of sight and invisible, because of the negative views of immigrants, racial and social profiling and discrimination, and the absence of a national immigration policy that recognizes the contributions of immigrants to the USA and establishes a positive context of reception (Stepick & Dutton Stepick, 2009). For instance, although rural multilingual families who are immigrants work on peanut farms, build houses and own commercial businesses, they have been portrayed as lazy, gangsters, drug addicts and thieves. Those stereotypes fail to recognize the contributions of immigrants to the USA.

Informal interviews

The American Civil Liberties Union (ACLU) worked with educators in the US state of Maine, which is a large rural state that is home to thousands of migrant workers who harvest crops such as apples and pears, and who supply food throughout the USA. Maine also has a large immigrant population in and beyond its larger cities – Portland and Bangor. In that state and unlike many US states, Spanish is not the most common language of multilingual students. Rather, Spanish follows Somali and Arabic in terms of speakers of other languages (Ruiz Soto *et al.*, 2015).

After learning that discriminatory practices had been taking place in the state, particularly with Muslim students, the ACLU conducted more than 100 interviews with parents, students, teachers and administrators. Particularly among multilingual students, the ACLU found that bullying and exclusion from school events were widespread and students of color faced an unwelcoming experience in schools (ACLU, 2017). Their report, 'We belong here: Eliminating inequity in education for immigrants and students of color in Maine', noted, 'consistent patterns of race-, religion-, and language-based exclusion and harassment across Maine schools' (ACLU, 2017: 13).

Consistent with what we find in rural settings, multilingual parents in Maine were deeply concerned and committed to the education of their children, but they found it difficult to engage with schools. One reason was that schools planned their events around middle class, nine-to-five work schedules, or did not provide multilingual support such as interpreters and translators for the school events. Another problem was that educators relied on children to interpret at meetings and to translate school materials, which caused a stressful experience for parents and placed uneven responsibility on children, disrupting the parent–child relationship. In order to mitigate those problems, the ACLU of Maine recommended among other things a 'consistent provision of professional interpreters' (ACLU, 2017: 44).

Maine is one example of how a state attempted to understand stereotypes surrounding immigrant, migrant and multilingual students in rural settings. We will review the ACLU's (2017) 'Empowered Parent and Family Engagement Manifesto' in the following chapter. However, the ACLU's use of interviews with a wide range of educators, families and students provided the input and awareness needed to understand negative stereotypes in specific ways, in order to begin to combat and redress those problems for students in schools.

In your school or district, how might you come to understand local stereotypes? Can you identify four to six families and conduct informal interviews with them, similar to the work of the ACLU in Maine? Gaining access to multilingual families will require some investigation into the backgrounds, experiences, languages and literacies of families, following your findings from Table 4.1.

To gain access to families, identify a cultural and linguistic liaison, or a person who can bridge the 'ontological distance' noted earlier by Domínguez (2017). A liaison may be a bilingual student aide or paraprofessional working at the school who is trusted by families. It could also be a key community member who has rapport within the community and with families. Remember that your cultural or linguistic liaison might not be a member of your staff or school. An informed liaison will have connections to families and understands local languages used in homes, labor practices and times of work, and who in the homes is responsible for the children's education.

As noted above in our exploration of 'who families are', another key way to learn about families is to speak with children directly, speak with families, and invite them and extended family members to a school or community event. Asking families and children what languages they speak at home, their histories, what their favourite stories are, how their local networks work, and what access to media and literacy events they have are important intake information and contribute to a more accurate representation or awareness of rural multilingual families.

Observations

Educators can learn about rural multilingual families by observing students as they arrive to school and how they interact in the school setting and events outside of the school. For example, children may be dropped off in the morning by people other than parents, such as grandparents or extended family. Children may walk or may take public transportation. Others may take boats (see Figure 4.1). How the children access the school provides insight into how parents or caregivers may need to access the school for events and support. Refer to Figures 4.2 and 4.3 as rural, international school settings. Take an 'inventory' of your school as a welcoming space, using simple observation techniques. Begin by looking at the school entranceway and door (see Figures 4.4 and 4.5). What imagery do you see and what message does it convey to families at school? Does the school staff smile? Are there visual images in multiple languages that greet families? Are there bilingual maps and materials for families to pick up such as the bilingual resource guide described earlier in this book? Are

Figure 4.1 Rural setting Ireland
Source: Maria Coady

Figure 4.2 Rural school South Africa
Source: Maria Coady

Figure 4.3 Rural school South Africa
Source: Maria Coady

Figure 4.4 Rural school Florida, USA
Source: Maria Coady

Figure 4.5 Rural school Florida, USA
Source: Maria Coady

the images reflective of people in the community or are they a more 'standard' and traditional image of family stereotypes?

What Multilingual Families Experience at the School Door

A good way to build rural multilingual family engagement is to ensure that everyone, especially multilingual families who have traveled purposefully to your school, is greeted at the school door by staff who are prepared to do so in a language the families speak. This means ensuring that staff welcome families warmly and greet them in a language the families know. Welcome signs are visual examples of how families may feel welcomed in the school and ways that their languages are affirmed. Using multiple languages literally tell families that they are valued and that the school wants to communicate and build relationships with them. As part of building a linguistically-responsive school environment, school faculty and staff could identify and learn phrases of welcome, support and engagement in multiple languages. This step cannot be overlooked in seeking to gain trust and respect of families and building a relationship that invites them in through the school door. It demonstrates that the school staff genuinely cares about families' cultures and knowledges, as Ladson-Billings (1994) described earlier.

In addition, is the school's physical layout easy to understand? Families need to know how the school is arranged, where their children attend classes, where they eat and how they get home in the afternoon after school ends. The first time parents arrive at school, ensure that the staff can provide a map, written in multiple languages with school icons (e.g. restrooms, book symbol for a library or a computer for a media center). I attended a recent 'back to school night' at a rural school district, where multilingual families had to locate the school cafeteria, identify the child's teacher on a list of all teachers in the cafeteria and then find their way to the classroom to meet the teacher. The new, multilingual families were confused, lost and felt marginalized, and unwelcome in the school.

Families who do not know how the school functions or their way around the school describe feeling like second-class citizens (Mancilla, 2017). In the US state of Washington, parents were invited to be part of a panel of parent voices. Parents on the panel were asked to describe their experiences with family engagement at school. They noted their sense of feeling invisible in schools and they discussed how they experienced a deficit ideology from schools, never quite sure how schools function, including having very limited communication with their children's teachers. Instead of teachers talking to parents, this panel did the opposite: parents essentially 'taught' the teachers about their experiences, their desires for their children and their need to engage with schools.

Rural schools might have school campuses that are physically large spaces, because rural school districts combine students across grade levels, reducing the need for multiple school buildings. If you were to walk through the hallways, the cafeteria or the school parking lot, how welcoming is the school environment for rural multilingual families? Can multiple languages be used in the school signage? Can icons or symbol be used to ensure that the classroom grade levels are clear?

Students from multilingual backgrounds can work with teachers to develop artwork, signs and cultural icons that represent their families, including families that have two mothers, fathers or nonbiological parents. Images can be displayed on school walls, in the office, at the school library or media center, even at the school entrance before families enter. In addition, students can contribute to the visual environment of the school in ways by developing and translating school signs in their home languages.

Conclusion

This chapter focused on how our personal family stories serve to inform our views of families in education. We challenge some existing assumptions and stereotypes about traditional or nontraditional family configurations, languages and functioning, particularly with images from the media. Learning about multilingual families can take multiple forms, but teachers and educators can learn by connecting family's strengths of language and culture and connecting those to specific school-based learning tasks and activities. Finally, we explored the way schools are configured to welcome (or not) families into the school site and the languages that are used.

Activities

Activity 1

Take a field trip with a colleague in your school. Start your field trip at the approach to the school. What do you notice? Are signs and information given in languages that parents speak? If parents are nonliterate in the home languages, what symbols and icons represent the school, directions for entering the school and arrows or other symbols for entering?

Draw a map as you walk from the road into the school area. Highlight areas of the school entrance where you might create symbols or multilingual signs to assist families in finding the school office. Once they arrive at the front office door, what are they expected to do? Who greets them and how? What languages and school images are families exposed to right away, upon initial entry into the school?

Finally, what role does the school front desk administrator play in welcoming families to school? Does the school staff have materials, including an oral or multilingual script, that they can point to or say when families arrive? If a new rural multilingual family enters the school and does not speak the school language or language of the staff, how are interpreters accessed or appointments made for when families return?

End your field trip with a list of suggestions of three or four items you can produce, translate or change that will help rural multilingual families access the school and make them feel welcome and supported in their languages and cultures. Share your findings with colleagues. Write a short action plan – 2 or 3 suggestions – for building a culturally- and linguistically-responsive environment for rural multilingual families.

Activity 2 (adapted from Staehr Fenner & Snyder, 2017)

Reflecting on cultural beliefs and assumptions

The table below shows cultural beliefs and assumptions about education that differ across cultural groups. Examine and describe your personal and/or group cultural beliefs of education using the table below as a guide.

Topic	Your beliefs and/or expectations
Role of teacher	
Role of the student	
Punctuality	
Student participation in class discussions through language(s)	
Independent versus collaborative learning*	
Plagiarism	

Share your table with colleagues.

- How are these topics reflective of cultural values and assumptions?
- What topics are 'missing' from this table related to education?
- How might cultural beliefs differ for rural multilingual families, immigrant families and migrant families?

References

American Civil Liberties Union of Maine (ACLU) (2017) We belong here: Eliminating inequity in education for immigrants and students of color in Maine. See https://www.aclumaine.org/en/publications/report-we-belong-here.

Christiansen, L. (1998) Where I'm from. *Rethinking Schools*. See https://www.rethinkingschools.org/articles/where-i-m-from.

Coady, M., Harper, C. and de Jong, E. (2016) Aiming for equity: Preparing mainstream teachers for inclusion or inclusive classrooms? *TESOL Quarterly* 50 (2), 340–368. DOI: 10.1002/tesq.223

Domínguez, M. (2017) 'Se hace puentes al andar': Decolonial teacher education as a needed bridge to culturally sustaining and revitalizing pedagogies. In D. Paris and H.S. Alim (eds) *Culturally Sustaining Pedagogies: Teaching and Learning for Justice in a Changing World* (pp. 225–246). New York: Teachers College Press.

Edgell, P. and Docka, D. (2007) Beyond the nuclear family? Familism and gender ideology in diverse religious commuities. *Sociological Forum* 22 (1), 26–51. DOI: 10.1111/j.1573-7861.2006.00003.x

Fadiman, A. (1998) *The Spirit Catches You and You Fall Down*. New York: Farrar, Straus, & Giroux Publishers.

Gargiulo, R.M. and Bouck, E.C. (2017) *Special Education in Contemporary Society: An Introduction to Exceptionality* (6th edn). Thousand Oaks, CA: Sage.

Ladson-Billings, G. (1994) *The Dreamkeepers: Successful Teachers of African American Children*. San Francisco: Jossey-Bass.

Lyon, G.E. (1993) Where I'm From. See http://www.georgeellalyon.com/where.html.

Mancilla, L. (2017) *Engaging with Families of English Learners*. Presentation at the National WIDA Conference. Oct. 16–19. Tampa, FL.

Makalela, L. (2015) Translanguaging as a vehicle for epistemic access: Cases for reading comprehension and multilingual interactions. *Per Linguam* 31 (1), 15–29. http://dx.doi.org/10.5785/31-1-628

Olivos, E.M., Jiménez-Castellanos, O. and Ochoa, A.M. (2011) *Bicultural Parent Engagement: Advocacy and Empowerment*. New York: Teachers College Press.

Ruiz Soto, A.G., Hooker, S. and Batalova, J. (2015) *Top Languages Spoken by English Language Learners Nationally and by State*. Washington, DC: Migration Policy Institute. See https://www.migrationpolicy.org/research/top-languages-spoken-english-language-learners-nationally-and-state.

Sleeter, C. (2011) *Making Choices for Multicultural Education: Five Approaches to Race, Class and Gender* (6th edn). New York: Wiley.

Staehr Fenner, D. and Snyder, S. (2017). *Unlocking English Learners' Potential: Strategies for Making Content Accessible*. Thousand Oaks, CA: Corwin.

Stepick, A. and Dutton Stepick, C. (2009) Contexts of reception and feelings of belonging. *Forum: Qualitative Social Research* 10 (3), Art 15. http://www.qualitative-research.net/index.php/fqs/article/view/1366/2862.

Zentella, A.M. (2005) Premises, promises, and pitfalls of language socialization research in Latino families and communities. In A.M. Zentella (ed.) *Building on Strength: Language and Literacy in Latino Families and Communities* (pp. 13–30). New York: Teachers College Press.

5 Practice and Praxis: *Acting* to Engage Multilingual Families in Rural Schools

Highlights

- Linguistically-responsive family engagement.
- Preparing to engage rural multilingual families.
- Working with rural multilingual families throughout the year.
- Engaging rural multilingual families in school leadership.
- Activities for further learning.

Real Scenario

It is Monday night at a rural elementary school, and school begins for students on Thursday morning. Tonight is the school's annual 'Back to School Bash'. Teachers and school staff have been hard at work for four days already, anxiously anticipating the students' arrival and the beginning of the school year. The teachers have engaged in two full days of professional development (PD) at the school, some of which included how to access students data on the district's new online data system, a new teacher evaluation model that is being implemented in the school district and reviewing the new curriculum. They have also worked to prepare their classrooms and the cafeteria space, where tonight families will come to the school and line up according to their child's last name. Once in line, families will receive a large, neon green sheet of paper with the name of the student's homeroom teacher. From there, families will walk through the school to locate their child's classroom and meet the teacher.

Ms Rodriguez is a new, first grade teacher at the school. She painstakingly prepares her classroom for her 22 students, 13 girls and nine boys. The classroom walls display colorful images of letters and numbers, and the bookshelves are organized by topics. The small desks are arranged in groups that form small tables, because Ms Rodriguez anticipates using a lot of collaborative groupwork throughout the school year.

Ms Rodriguez creates three documents for the Back to School Bash: a sign in sheet for families which asks for the parent's name, the child's name, the parent's telephone number and the home address. The document is created with large boxes so that there is plenty of space for parents to write the information in the boxes. The second document is a repeat of the parent's and student's names, but asks parents to write the pickup plan for the student, indicating either 'car' or the student's bus number.

Across the room is a packet of papers arranged on clipboards that the parents are asked to complete to become a classroom 'Mystery Reader.' A Mystery Reader is a special guest who comes to the classroom to read a story to the students. Mystery Readers come to the class every week or so, depending on the volunteer's schedule. The students are always very excited to have a guest come to the class to read a special story and they also like guessing who the reader will be based on the clues. The questionnaire also asks for parents to write down their available times when they can come to the school to read to the first-grade students.

Sarita arrives at the school with her mother and father. She was a kindergartner at the school the prior year, but she is confused with all of the new faces and activities in the cafeteria. She is wearing her very best clothing, with golden sandals (*dorados*) and a long white crinoline skirt. Her black hair is combed back neatly. Her parents, Minerva and José, speak no English, but they gravitate to the bilingual paraprofessionals whom they recognize from Sarita's kindergarten year. They ask for help getting the green paper. Once they receive the teacher's name, they begin to search for Ms Rodriguez's classroom. It is a 10-minute walk to the other side of the large school campus. There are portable classrooms and several different buildings to navigate through. Eventually, they find the correct building, following arrows and signage that says 'ALL FIRST GRADERS →' They cannot read the sign, but they guess at what it says and continue to follow the arrows through the school.

The family enters the classroom and are greeted by Ms Rodriguez who bends down to Sarita and ask her name. 'Sara', the first grader replies softly. A small smile grows on her face. Ms Rodriguez stands and asks Sarita's mother, 'What is your name?' but Minerva does not respond. She looks down quietly and embarrassed. Her husband stands quietly three feet behind her.

Not sure what to do, Ms Rodriguez points to the sign in sheets on the table at the doorway of the classroom and indicates to the parents that they should fill in the boxes. Minerva approaches the papers with trepidation and looks down at the forms and the blue pen, then back up at the teacher who has moved on to greet other families entering the classroom and who have questions about the Mystery Reader questionnaire.

Introduction

Unfortunately, this scenario is not unusual in classrooms each year where rural multilingual families bring their children to meet the teacher, learn about the school and become familiar with the child's classroom. In rural settings, families have planned and traveled distances to get to school in the evening before the school year. Yet for both Sarita's parents and Ms Rodriguez, this event was not what either had anticipated. Ms Rodriguez felt thwarted and perplexed that all of her work preparing her classroom for her students and families did not end with having the parents volunteer as Mystery Readers or completing the required information. She is still not sure if the mother or father can read and write in Spanish or English. In addition, she failed to get the student's pickup information and bus number, so she is nervous that Sarita might miss the bus after the first day of school. For Minerva, José and Sarita, the event also did not go well. Their excitement and anticipation of meeting the teacher left them feeling embarrassed, isolated and uneducated, a difficult start to a long school year.

In what ways did this short event not meet the needs of families or of schools? In what ways could this event be reimagined and reframed using a lens of critical and linguistically responsive pedagogy?

This chapter focuses on ways to act in linguistically responsive, family-centered ways for rural multilingual families. To *act* means to do something purposeful that will support the education of your multilingual students. Earlier we reviewed some key ideas related to preparing teachers and educators to be linguistically responsive to multilingual families. Note that acting in linguistically responsive ways is not simply about translating information and school communications into languages that parents or caregivers know. Rather, it is learning about the rich and varied backgrounds of families, where they are from, what they believe – especially about education – and strengths that they contribute to the home, school and local community. Often, their contributions go unacknowledged and remain invisible. Our task is to identify their contributions to the local environment and highlight their strengths. Linguistically responsive pedagogy includes the following foci:

- *Academic achievement and student learning* – In particular, multilingual students have access to a wide range of linguistic talents, resources and flexibility, and educators of multilingual students can work toward the use of students' multiple languages in their practice.
- *Linguistic competence* – Educators of multilingual students who engage families have some knowledge of the languages that their students speak. It is beneficial for educators to also have access to and knowledge of another language, even at a beginner level. Knowledge of more than one language – and how languages work – is an asset that educators can use, because it helps us to understand how multilinguals make sense of school, education and the world.

- *Sociopolitical competence* – This includes an awareness of the relationship between education and politics, the reality of life for families from various linguistic, ethnic, racial and cultural backgrounds. Education is an inherently social and political act. Teachers and school leaders make decisions every day about the language(s) they use for instruction, language(s) they use to engage families, as well as how they interact with other people outside of the school. In today's world, decisions about the language of assessment for multilingual students are paramount and affect how students are considered to be 'successful' in school.

Reimagine Sarita's new school year, but let us align the parent–teacher encounter and first school events to the three areas of Linguistically Responsive Pedagogy (LRP) described above. As you think about this, what changes and specific actions can the teacher take to ensure that rural, multilingual families are engaged with their child's education and learning?

Engaging Families *Before* They Arrive

Teachers are usually anxious and happy to meet students on the first day of school, or even before if the school hosts events to meet new students and families. However, learning about students must occur well before that event. In Chapter 4, we identified key information that educators need to be aware of before students and families arrive at school. Tables 4.2 and 4.3 are tools to help guide meeting with, preparing for and building trust with families. It is essential that educators initiate family engagement activities and then continuously follow through by recommunicating with them.

For example, from the scenario above, Ms Rodriguez can learn about Sarita's family, home languages, literacies and cultural background before the first day of school. She might learn about how the families arrived in the community and the work they engage in. She can understand how the community functions, its resources for food, shelter, transportation, medical and dental care. She can talk informally with her colleagues and Sarita's former teacher from kindergarten, and she can also seek input on community agencies that work with multilingual families. It is essential to know how to communicate with Sarita's family before the very first school event – like meet the teacher – and to have three or more different options available to communicate. One option is a bilingual educator who could facilitate the meeting. Another option is reduced-text information for parents. A third option is a bilingual text for families who are literate in the home language.

Families need key school and safety information right away, such as: who is my child's teacher, when does school open and close, how will my child eat, how will my child get to or from school and what happens when my child is sick? Immigrant multilingual families bring different educational experiences with them and their knowledge about the roles of school personnel differs. In addition, in rural settings one person may play

Who is Who in My Child's School
Quién es quien en la escuela de mi hijo/a

Director(a) – la persona encargada de la escuela, el/la líder
Director or Principal – the person in charge of the school, the school leader
Name/Nombre _____

Director(a) Asistente Subdirector(a)* – la persona encargada—en general—del comportamiento de los alumnos
Assistant Director or Vice Principal – the person sometimes in charge of student behavior in school
Name/Nombre _____

*In Mexico there is not an equivalent to Assistant Director but rather Subdirectores (like subdirector académico, etc).

Asistente bilingüe – una persona bilingüe que ayuda a el/la maestro(a)
Bilingual aide – a bilingual person or classroom aide who helps the teacher
Name/Nombre _____

Guidance Counselor Trabajador(a) social– una persona encargada de ayudar a mi hijo(a) en sus relaciones familiares y sociales, en sus amistades, así como en su horario escolar y orientación vocacional.
Guidance Counselor – the person in charge of helping my child with family, social, friend relationships, with her school schedule, and materials for further education.
Name/Nombre _____

Maestro(a) – la persona encargada del aprendizaje de mi hijo(a)
Teacher – the person in charge of my child's learning
Name/Nombre _____

Figure 5.1 Who's who in school (Rural Women's Health Project)

multiple roles – such as a 'newcomer' teacher, reading coach and head of transportation. A school guidance counselor, someone who might outreach to families and act as a student advocate, might also conduct specialized testing or assessments for students with learning disabilities. Those roles are likely not known to families, but Figure 5.1 is a sample of a reduced-text bilingual guide to school personnel and 'who's who' in my school.

Knowing who's who in the school is key to ensuring that rural multilingual families can communicate with the correct person. Often, multilingual families will rely on the one or two people in the school who speak their language even if that person does not attend the school.

Learning about my child's teachers and staff

In addition to learning the important people at school and who's who in the school structure, families need to know the different instructional staff of the student and how the child will be transported. On a given day, a student may have several different teachers, including a teacher for music or art, science and language learning. In rural schools, one teacher may fill all of those roles. However, when there is more than one teacher per school grade, teachers are able to specialize in a content area such as science and social studies/language arts, and children may have diff teachers responsible for different academic content.

Using imagery and languages in family communication

In some countries, families are requested to provide supplies for their children, such as uniforms, pencils and writing instruments, paper, and even books. Across the USA, many classroom teachers request items from families that will be used throughout the school year and shared by all of the children. As rural schools are under-resourced, teachers may ask families for eating utensils, basic medicines or hand sanitizer.

For multilingual families who have different educational experiences, providing supplies to classrooms may be at odds with their prior experiences of schools. In addition, they may not notice differences across types of writing instruments, washable versus unwashable glue or erasable pens. Different types of items might look similar but might not be what teachers and schools need. In our community, bilingual paraprofessionals prepare for families to meet the teacher at a 'Meet the Teacher Night' obtaining a list of the items that teachers requested. They generated an organizer for families that made it easy for them to identify the items. An example of the organizer is shown in Figure 5.2.

Working with Families Throughout the Year

Ongoing *school–home–school* communication

As noted earlier, rural multilingual family engagement is more about building sustainable relationships of trust and care with families than it is checking off a list of items that need to be accomplished. Organizing and planning for families to engage with the school is an ongoing, differentiated task that takes time and leadership.

In order to be engaged in their child's learning, there are some key things that rural multilingual families need to know, such as how the school functions, what days their child needs to attend school and the times to arrive and depart, changes to the school calendar, absentee policies when the child is sick and how they can communicate with educators when a child will be absent from school or other concerns arise. Families want to know what they can do to help their child at home, when important tests take place and what to do if a child faces trauma or bullying. While communication is generally thought of as a process of 'home–school communication', shifting this to a rural multilingual, differentiated and family-centered orientation means that schools learn about who families are first, what their needs are, and then initiate and sustain the kinds of interactions that are linguistically and culturally responsive to their needs. Schools also follow through with families with all communication.

ITEM/ARTICULO	
12 #2 pencils	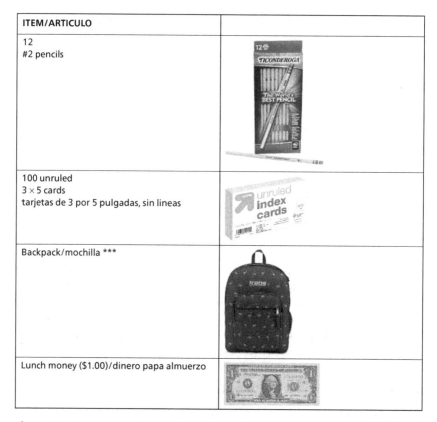
100 unruled 3 × 5 cards tarjetas de 3 por 5 pulgadas, sin lineas	
Backpack/mochilla ***	
Lunch money ($1.00)/dinero papa almuerzo	

Figure 5.2 Items needed for school

In other words, the school needs to identify, initiate, create, deliver and follow through in a cycle of communication throughout the year.

Schools can create a multilingual guide of resources for families that includes local information that can help them access services. This is especially important in rural settings where there are few resources. One drawback to printed materials is that guides need frequent updating because in migratory rural communities, both families and local resources also change frequently.

When identifying community resources for our multilingual families, we ensured that there were actual language-able (multilingual) staff or personnel working in those settings or agencies before we provided the information to families. We checked hours of operation and noted when a multilingual staff member would be available to answer phones or questions. We ensured that the language of the guide reflected the local varieties of language (including different varieties of Spanish) and that it was current, appropriate and made sense to rural multilingual families. In the local resource guide shown in Figure 5.3, notice icons and pictures are

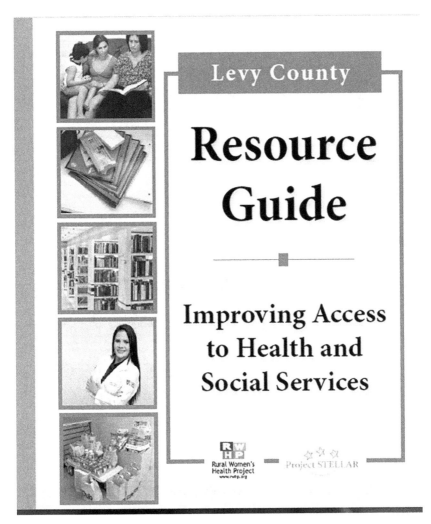

Figure 5.3 *Guia*/community resource guide
Source: Rural Women's Health Project (2017)

used to direct families to those places where there is a person who speaks the home language. Icons and other images are useful for multilingual families with nonwritten literacy backgrounds.

Simply sending the guide home, however, is not enough to ensure that rural multilingual families know how to use it and who to contact when something in the guide no longer works. Our community partners create a paper guide or *guía* for multilingual families with an instruction sheet for educators to learn how to use the guide with families. A sample of a multilingual resource guide for our rural community is shown in Figure 5.3.

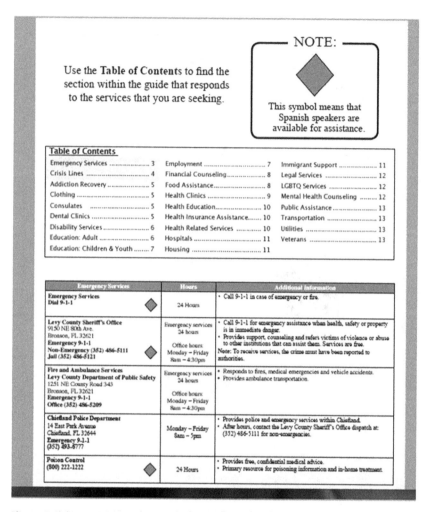

NOTE:

Use the **Table of Contents** to find the section within the guide that responds to the services that you are seeking.

This symbol means that Spanish speakers are available for assistance.

Table of Contents

Emergency Services	Hours	Additional Information
Emergency Services Dial 9-1-1	24 Hours	• Call 9-1-1 in case of emergency or fire.
Levy County Sheriff's Office 9150 NE 80th Ave. Bronson, FL 32621 Emergency 9-1-1 Non-Emergency (352) 486-5111 Jail (352) 486-5121	Emergency services 24 hours Office hours Monday – Friday 8am – 4:30pm	• Call 9-1-1 for emergency assistance when health, safety or property is in immediate danger. • Provides support, counseling and refers victims of violence or abuse to other institutions that can assist them. Services are free. Note: To receive services, the crime must have been reported to authorities.
Fire and Ambulance Services Levy County Department of Public Safety 1251 NE County Road 343 Bronson, FL 32621 Emergency 9-1-1 Office (352) 486-5209	Emergency services 24 hours Office hours Monday – Friday 8am – 4:30pm	• Responds to fires, medical emergencies and vehicle accidents. • Provides ambulance transportation.
Chiefland Police Department 14 East Park Avenue Chiefland, FL 32644 Emergency 9-1-1 (352) 493-8777	Monday – Friday 8am – 5pm	• Provides police and emergency services within Chiefland. • After hours, contact the Levy County Sheriff's Office dispatch at: (352) 486-5111 for non-emergencies.
Poison Control (800) 222-1222	24 Hours	• Provides free, confidential medical advice. • Primary resource for poisoning information and in-home treatment.

Figure 5.3 *(Continued)*

Parent–teacher conferences

Rural multilingual families who speak languages other than the school language generally feel intimidated when they arrive in schools and do not understand what is being said or the cultural norms of the school. They also may not ask for help, as with the Álvarez family, who chose to attend but remain silent in the back of the room. Multilingual families in rural settings face the challenge of time and distance, so asking parents or caregivers for a physical presence in school is a time-consuming task. Rather than being talked to with an overload of text and materials, identify places in the school or in the community where multilingual families are comfortable and bring student information to them. This may be at a

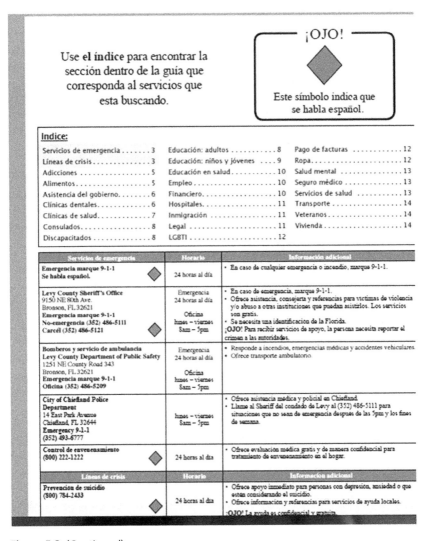

¡OJO!

Use **el indice** para encontrar la sección dentro de la guía que corresponda al servicios que esta buscando.

Este símbolo indica que se habla español.

Indice:

Servicios de emergencia 3	Educación: adultos 8	Pago de facturas 12
Líneas de crisis 3	Educación: niños y jóvenes 9	Ropa 12
Adicciones 5	Educación en salud 10	Salud mental 13
Alimentos 5	Empleo 10	Seguro médico 13
Asistencia del gobierno 6	Financiero 10	Servicios de salud 13
Clínicas dentales 6	Hospitales 11	Transporte 14
Clínicas de salud 7	Inmigración 11	Veteranos 14
Consulados 8	Legal 11	Vivienda 14
Discapacitados 8	LGBTI 12	

Servicios de emergencia	Horario	Información adicional
Emergencia marque 9-1-1 Se habla español.	24 horas al día	• En caso de cualquier emergencia o incendio, marque 9-1-1.
Levy County Sheriff's Office 9150 NE 80th Ave. Bronson, FL 32621 Emergencia marque 9-1-1 No-emergencia (352) 486-5111 Carcel (352) 486-5121	Emergencia 24 horas al día Oficina lunes – viernes 8am – 5pm	• En caso de emergencia, marque 9-1-1. • Ofrece asistencia, consejería y referencias para victimas de violencia y/o abuso a otras instituciones que puedan asistirlos. Los servicios son gratis. ¡OJO! Para recibir servicios de apoyo, la persona necesita reportar el crimen a las autoridades.
Bomberos y servicio de ambulancia Levy County Department of Public Safety 1251 NE County Road 343 Bronson, FL 32621 Emergencia marque 9-1-1 Oficina (352) 486-5209	Emergencia 24 horas al día Oficina lunes – viernes 8am – 5pm	• Responde a incendios, emergencias médicas y accidentes vehiculares. • Ofrece transporte ambulatorio.
City of Chiefland Police Department 14 East Park Avenue Chiefland, FL 32644 Emergency 9-1-1 (352) 493-6777	lunes – viernes 8am – 5pm	• Ofrece asistencia médica y policial en Chiefland • Llame al Sheriff del condado de Levy al (352) 486-5111 para situaciones que no sean de emergencia después de las 5pm y los fines de semana.
Control de envenenamiento (800) 222-1222	24 horas al día	• Ofrece evaluación médica gratis y de manera confidencial para tratamiento de envenenamiento en el hogar.

Líneas de crisis	Horario	Información adicional
Prevención de suicidio (800) 784-2433	24 horas al día	• Ofrece apoyo inmediato para personas con depresión, ansiedad o que están considerando el suicidio. • Ofrece información y referencias para servicios de ayuda locales. ¡OJO! La ayuda es confidencial y gratuita.

Figure 5.3 *(Continued)*

community center, a church, a shopping space or a library. Once there, always begin by asking families what they would like to know, how, in what ways, by which mediums (oral, written, electronic) and in which languages. Plan for additional time allocated for multilingual families, particularly if translation and interpretation services are being used.

Our experience with rural multilingual families is that they will attend schools when their child's learning is being discussed, as with the parent–teacher conference nights, and when their child is performing in a school dance, play, skit or other activity. In those cases, we have found parents present and engaged in their child's education. Unfortunately, many of the school materials and reporting systems today are technical and literacy-based. Reading a report card is a cultural event that is often confusing to both multilingual and monolingual families. And when there are translations of school grades and reporting materials, families may not understand how to interpret them.

In today's high-tech environment, even rural schools use media to convey outcomes from student learning. I hear teachers engage with parents regarding their child's academic performance on software programs such as iReady or WIDA language proficiency test scores. Using academic terminology to convey student learning is likely to not make sense to families, and even more so with families from other countries where these programs are not used. As with using sound instructional strategies to make language and content comprehensible to multilingual children in schools, educators must find ways to make student performance, behavior and academic success comprehensible to parents.

Preparing for meetings

Educators frequently do not realize that they speak the language of education, or 'education-ese' that includes technical terminology, acronyms and phrases that are only known to educators. The names of tests, for example, can be confusing. For instance, in the USA there are multiple English language proficiency examinations to determine the language ability of students. The acronyms of the tests include: LAB, LAS, IPT, IELTS, TOEFL, ACCESS, BVAT and so on. Using acronyms and other education terminology related to student learning programs such as Snap and Read, iReady and Edgenuity need to be unpacked by describing the purpose of those assessments and made comprehensible to families in languages they know and using their cultural background as references. Identify different ways to describe the work that multilingual students do and how that child is performing using everyday language that parents can understand. Additional suggestions for rural multilingual family engagement meetings include:

(1) *Avoid education jargon, acronyms and terminology.* In the field of education, there are many acronyms and educational jargon that teacher share in their daily work. However, families generally have no knowledge of these terminologies. They feel alienated and lost when they attend meetings where the focus is to convey information to the families regarding their child's learning.

(2) *Build on multilingual families' strengths of language and culture.* Recognize that families bring those resources to the school and community, and ensure that students' backgrounds, cultures and languages are visible and integrated in school classrooms, hallways, offices, books and the curriculum. Multilingual children and parents

who see themselves represented in the school's materials and hear their languages spoken can see themselves as participants and partners in the education of their children. In contrast, parents who see themselves in stereotypes and whose language and voices are invisible in the school will not likely engage in school-based events.

(3) *Prepare for the meeting(s) before families arrive.* Bilingual paraprofessionals or trained interpreters must meet with teachers and/or principals before the families attend a parent–teacher meeting. Interpreters may not know the exact terminology or ways to translate technical information to parents, nor the cultural assumptions surrounding issues such as special educational services for children, educational assessments and evaluation, and social emotional support for children that may be needed. *Children should not be used as interpreters or translators during parent–teacher meetings or for communicating school information and business.* The use of children disrupts the child–parent relationship.

(4) *Prepare to follow up with multilingual families.* For each meeting you hold, identify the next steps that need to be taken. For example, if parents or caregivers did not understand their child's reading scores, identify ways to follow up using imagery, cultural informants, or interpreters or translations so that they are not left guessing and wondering what they missed. In addition, plan and prepare for the next family–teacher meeting. Are there different family members who might attend? What nights work best for families? Can they access transportation for each planned meeting? These are just some of the ways educators can ensure that there is school–home–school communication.

Helping families to understand (the culture of) assessment

In our rural community, we recognized that all families had difficulty reading student report cards and interpreting their grades, but this was especially true for multilingual families. We also knew that families' social networking consisted of *promotoras* who were key members that conveyed information to families across the rural community. The cultural background of families was predominantly Latino, with families coming from vastly different Latino cultures: Puerto Rican, Venezuelan, Mexican and Guatemalan. We created and assessed the use of *fotonovelas*, or graphic novels, to convey information with families regarding how they could understand their children's school report cards. An example is shown in Figure 5.4.

Once we created the materials, we strategically worked in the school media center during the parent–teacher conference night when students' grades were being discussed. Interpreters were available along with bilingual volunteers. Each family was given a *fotonovela* that showed how to read the report card and was shown how the to relate the *fotonovela* to the actual report card of the child. Like the multilingual resource guide of

Figure 5.4 *Como lo leo*/How to read the report card
Source: Maria Coady

community services above, engagement consists of working alongside multilingual families to communicate their child's learning.

The *fotonovelas* were culturally- and linguistically-responsive to the families in our rural community using the languages that they spoke. For example, we knew that there was a migration network of multilingual families. Culturally, graphic novels or picture novels made the most sense to use because they were familiar to families. As we created the materials, we took care not to stereotype families, but rather to connect ways of communicating with school-based information. We also knew that technology-based communications would be less successful, because

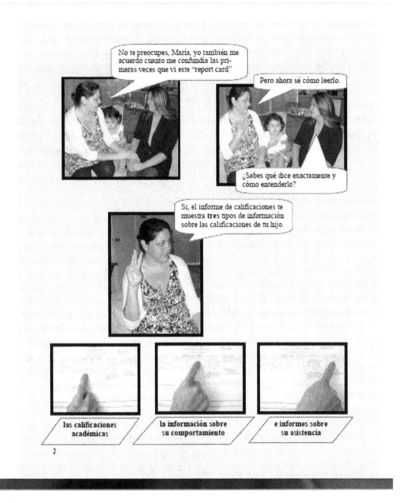

Figure 5.4 (*Continued*)

families preferred to meet in person. Other communities may be less contact-rich and artifacts such as *fotonovelas* may be less helpful for families. Moreover, in some cultures, images of a woman would not be used and men may be more appropriately depicted in imagery. Families' backgrounds and languages should inform the creation and dissemination of school-based materials, especially in order for engagement to be appropriate and family-centered.

Building on home literacies

Educators often do not know which literacy practices are used in the homes of their students. Sometimes families engage in oral storytelling as a form of knowledge and literacy, as well as a way to convey important cultural and historic information that is passed down across generations. In a prior study (Coady, 2009), I studied the home literacy practices of a Spanish-speaking family living in a rural community.

Alvarez (2017) describes one family literacy building project that took place in a first-grade classroom in a USA–Mexico border community. In the project, bilingual families shared their home languages, cultures and backgrounds while generating familial books, called *senderos familiares* or family trails. For example, in this event, families related a particular event, story or aspect of their family history in any language that they know. Alvarez describes how the family book project unearthed families' desires to hold on to their home culture and languages. At the same time, children were developing 'simultaneous identities' as they engaged in school and home literacy practices.

Nieto (2017) describes a similar multilingual literacy event where families – parents and caregivers in collaboration with their children – created a family timeline that described stories to present to their class. The family timelines included artifacts, stories and histories of families. Nieto suggests that schools move beyond decrying parents 'not showing up' and become creative, innovative, reflective and affirming in ways that engage multilingual families to support student learning in and out of school. Other creative examples may be bilingual, multilingual family book nights or book clubs, where families can meet monthly and share bilingual or multilingual books, using the school as a hub for literacy.

Using technology to engage rural multilingual families

Technology is ubiquitous in today's global world. Generally, in rural settings there is cellular service and access to some technologies to communicate, but they are not always reliable. While the internet is not stable and is expensive for families to provide, schools can use cell phone numbers as resources to connect with families. For example, schools, community leaders or a parent can create subgroups of parents that share languages to establish a support network, share school information and share transportation to school events. Educators who have access to the languages families read and write can use the cell phone-based parent community to text simple messages and reminders to parents.

Our community partner created a similar text-chain for multilingual families in our rural school district. They used cell phone numbers to create a social network to share information regarding meetings and local events such as talks on immigration, food security and labor. They were vigilant about not sharing individuals' phone numbers and the names were removed from their dataset to ensure privacy. They also did not over-use the system and sent infrequent reminder messages to families.

Engaging Families in School Leadership

Ultimately, our goal is to be in trusting and caring relationships with families where they are not an off-shoot of the school, but rather they *are* the school. Engaged families bring different ways of knowing and contributing to the multilingual, multicultural identity of the school. Families, then, need to be part of the decision-making processes of the school. Across some cultural groups, this may seem to be an unusual relationship (Coady & Yilmaz, 2017). We need more space for families' voices, experiences and ideas in order to have active and effective rural multilingual family engagement.

Some school districts have generated a 'Family Engagement Mission Statement' that describes the role of all families in the school leadership and school culture. For schools with diverse multilingual, multicultural families, the mission statement should be inclusive of all families. An example of a Family Engagement Mission Statement is

Through preparation and systemic support, our school will work with every family to support the equitable education and academic achievement of their children in all languages and across all cultures. Parent and caregiver support is based on the needs of families alongside the school's goals for student learning.

As part of their outreach, the ACLU worked with schools to create a 'Parent Manifesto' in their report, 'We Belong Here' (ACLU, 2017). Some of the recommendations that related to rural multilingual families included:

(1) Language access – a consistent provision of professional interpreters is crucial to successful parent outreach.
(2) Events for immigrant families – programs and events should be specifically tailored to families' needs and publicized widely in multiple languages.
(3) Empowering marginalized parent voices – successful communication, active listening and structurally empowering families to participate in school policies, programs and conversations.

They noted that families who 'come from authoritarian countries may not fully understand their right to have a say in their children's education' (ACLU, 2017: 47), and educators must ensure that families know how to request or reject services and programs for their children.

Conclusion

In sum, educators must view rural multilingual families from a strengths-based perspective where parents and caregivers may hold different views of the concept of 'education' and 'teacher' than mainstream parents. Here we advocate for 'school–home–school' communication that is culturally and linguistically appropriate and sensitive to the rural nature of schools and families, and schools should always follow up with families. In educational contexts, teachers discover students' and families' home languages and cultures; affirm students' identities through the curricular and instructional decisions that they make; and enhance rural multilingual families' strengths by using their knowledge and experiences as resources.

Activities

Activity 1

Review the goals and materials in this chapter. Identify two of the materials presented (such as Who's Who in my Child's School, *Como Lo Leo*/How to Read the Report Card). Review them carefully. In what ways will this material meet the needs of your multilingual families? How could these materials be adapted? Are there additional languages or cultural resources that are more appropriate for your community?

Activity 2

Review the Family Engagement Mission Statement in this chapter. Write one for your school. How can you identify, invite and support families to participate in writing the mission statement? In what languages will it be written? What specific multilingual or literacy goals can you set forth in the mission statement? Where will you display your mission statement?

References

ACLU (2017) We belong here: Eliminating inequity in education for immigrants and students of color in Maine. See https://www.aclumaine.org/en/publications/report-we-belong-here.

Alvarez, A. (2017) Senderos familiars: Building pedagogical pathways to advance strength-based perspectives and inclusive family engagement in bilingual classrooms. Unpublished doctoral dissertation. University of Colorado, Boulder.

Coady, M. (2009) '*Solamente libros importantes*': Literacy practices and ideologies of migrant farmworking families in north central Florida. In G. Li (ed.) *Multicultural Families, Home Literacies and Mainstream Schooling* (pp. 113–128). Charlotte, NC: New Age.

Coady, M.R. and Yilmaz, T. (2017) Preparing teachers of ELs: Home-school partnerships. *TESOL Encyclopedia of English Language Teaching*. Hoboken, NJ: Wiley.

Nieto, D. (2017) Panel on family engagement. National WIDA Conference. Oct. 16–19. Tampa, FL.

Rural Women's Health Project (2017) See www.rwhp.org.

6 The Intersectionality of Rurality, Poverty and Immigration for Latino Families in the USA

> 'The bottom line is, all of it affects our kids.'
> Rural high school principal on the sociopolitical
> context of education (2018)

Highlights

- Undocumented immigrants.
- Ecological social systems theory.
- Latino families' support for child learning.
- Activities for further learning.

Introduction

Largely hidden from public view, the estimated 11 million undocumented[1] immigrants living in the USA comprise the backbone of many of the US's industries, including construction and building, crop industry and agriculture, restaurant, hotel, landscape, home care and day laborers (Passel & Cohn, 2016). Economists predict that without immigrant labor, many US states would face devastating economic consequences (Kurtzleben, 2013). The Pew Research Center estimates that 52% of undocumented persons in the US emigrate from Mexico, but they predict further that the number of undocumented Mexicans is estimated to shift downward over the next 20 years (Passel & Cohn, 2016). The US-based Migration Policy Institute, which tracks undocumented migration flows in and out of the US, estimates that about 5.1 million US children under the age of 18 live with an undocumented parent, representing about 30%

---

[1] I use undocumented here over the pejorative term 'illegal'.

of all children of immigrants. And about 75% of children with an undocumented parent live below the federal poverty level (Capps *et al.*, 2016).

In recent years, rural settings have become nontraditional locales for immigrant multilingual families. Suro and Singer (2013) describe these as 'new destination' settings, where issues of rurality, English language acquisition and poverty intersect. Overall, rural settings comprise about 20% of all public school students in the USA (Strange *et al.*, 2012). In the state of Florida, which has 67 school districts, 20 of those districts (or about 30%) were considered to be rural (National Center for Education Statistics, 2017).

In addition, rural schools face an extreme lack of resources, including time, money and effective professional development for teachers. For example, in our rural Florida school district where families represent diverse countries across Latin America such as Venezuela, Guatemala, Mexico and Nicaragua, local school district funding is severely depressed. This is because local property taxes contribute to the overall school revenue base, a common funding scheme for schools across the USA (National Public Radio, 2016). However, in rural settings, owners of farmland of 20 acres or greater pay fewer taxes than the average homeowner on their agricultural land. Thus, the already-stressed tax base for rural schools is even more suppressed because farmland generates much less revenue for the schools. Third, families and communities are geographically distant, making family engagement for linguistically and culturally diverse difficult. Hansen-Thomas notes the 'culture clash' (2018: 2) and racial tensions that exacerbate home–school partnerships.

These issues – immigration and rurality – affect the education of thousands of children across the USA, and as the principal of a rural secondary school in a high poverty school district noted above, all of these issues affect children and their school experiences. Anxiety and stress follow issues of food security, immigration, access to work, healthcare and transportation. What do educators in the USA need to know about the intersection of rurality, poverty and immigration, particularly for Latino families? How can educators respond to the needs of undocumented children and their families in the context of education?

This chapter situates broad national narratives of these areas – rurality, poverty and immigration – using an ecological social systems framework derived from the work of Bronfenbrenner (1994) and Lemke (2000). I describe the interplay of these, arguing that despite the presence of these among Latino children and families in the USA, they affect families in different ways, even within the same rural community and school. I also review recent literature on family engagement with Latino families and conclude the chapter with a charge for more delineated and detailed research in this area. These issues underscore the need to differentiate family engagement and issue a call to educators that we can no longer separate education from the sociopolitical context in the USA.

Ecological Social Systems Theory

Two main ecological social systems theories help to frame and capture the relationship between the phenomena of poverty, rurality and immigration discourses that are increasingly pervasive in everyday discourse in the USA. Bronfenbrenner's (1979) ecological social systems theory was first introduced in the 1970s in the context of the field of developmental psychology. His work aimed to capture the multiple forces that came into play in terms of child development. Some of those forces were considered 'proximal processes' (Bronfenbrenner, 1994: 38). Proximal processes are all of the activities that are proximal or close to the child as they develop. Some examples include parent–child and child–child interactions that have a strong direct influence on child development. Other processes also come into play, namely, increasingly broader environmental or systemic influences that surround the child at various levels (see Figure 6.1).

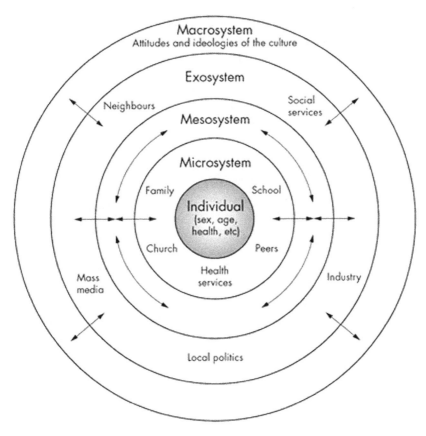

Figure 6.1 Reproduced with permission from Bronfenbrenner's ecological social systems theory (1994)

Five systems characterize Bronfenbrenner's ecological social systems theory, which, he argues, affect individual child development. The five systems include the microsystem, mesosystem, exosystem, macrosystem and chronosystem. These are increasingly broader spheres that influence the development of a child.

At the inner most circle is the child, located within a microsystem. The microsystem is the immediate environment in which the individual closely interacts with others. This can be a classroom, a home, a community center or religious institution. In these microsystem locations, interactions take place between the child and other people. Immediately outside of the individual is a level described as a mesosystem. In the mesosystem, two or more microsystems interact. These consist of connections that take place between, for example, the school and home, which is much of the focus of this book. Importantly, both settings are central to the developing child. The exosystem comprises the third system, which is characterized as links between a social setting where the individual does not have an active role and the individual's immediate context. One example may be work and schools, the latter of which the individual has direct experiences. Thus the mesosystem involves one setting that does not contain the developing child as actively participating in it.

The last two systems are the macrosystem and the chronosystem. The macrosystem reflects a wider social, political or cultural context that affects children's cultural norms and values. It includes knowledge and ways of knowing customs, lifestyles and beliefs. The value afforded education, for example, and the belief that to be educated (*bien educado*) reflects being well-behaved and respectful as an example of those. Other broad narratives such as social discourses surrounding what poverty is, who immigrants are and so forth exist within this system. The chronosystem encompasses changes over time in an environment as well as changes over time in a person or child. The effects of immigration policies on a family over time will affect the decision-making of the family that affects the child.

Suárez-Orozco *et al.* (2010) describe multiple overlapping ecological contexts that influence immigrant multilingual students in secondary schools in the USA. For instance, on an individual level, the challenges students face might include,

> [finding] themselves stripped of many key relationships – close friends, extended family, and familiar community members – and find themselves in a new social context where customs, schools, and (often) the language are different in both striking and subtle ways. (Suárez-Orozco *et al.*, 2010: 16)

Not all ecological social systems have the same influence on a child. Lemke (2000), for example, noted the importance of the time dimension in Bronfenbrenner's ecological framework, asking, 'What's happening?' at any given moment. For example, in a school classroom each utterance and activity happens in a context and time. Some timescales are short, such as a single utterance, comment or response to a teachers' question, while other activities span long-term processes. In the context of education, for example, the school building and classroom design, a curriculum that spans across multiple years or decades, and even the layout of the students' seats in a room affect the educational environment and learning experiences of student. The contribution of time in relation to Bronfenbrenner's ecological social systems theory reminds us that the broader narratives in which educators work, and within which multilingual families function, are not only sensitive to past, current and future policies and practices, but that they fluctuate, move and have an impact on students in multiple ways.

Hamman's (2018) work in bilingual education, two-way immersion (TWI) programs, where two languages are used as mediums of instruction, highlights the 'ideological flows' that move between the ecological systems and that ultimately affect the student. Hamman describes the center of the eco-social model that situates the student and his or her experiences. That is, how the student experiences education in the center system is influenced by increasingly larger systems. Surrounding the student is the TWI or bilingual classroom. In the classroom, class-level language policies, practices and teacher pedagogies occur, though arguably these are enacted by classroom teachers and school staff who hold views about bilingual education and student learning. At the next level, the school within which the TWI classroom is housed, influences the student and itself reflects the bilingual program model and a cadre of bilingual teachers. Educators and school leaders, parents and other stakeholders influence the bilingual program through their ideologies and actions, which continue to influence the student's experiences.

At the next level, state and district policies surrounding bilingualism and bilingual education affect the school and how it functions. Finally, national and global ideologies and the sociopolitical discourses interact with state and district policies. To the degree that these are large narratives that are negotiated over time, this level of the eco-social model relates to Bronfenbrenner's chronosystem.

Multiple and often competing discourses interact at the various ecological social layers that frame and influence teachers' and educators' everyday decisions surrounding multilingual children and families living in rural settings. The current sociopolitical context of education for children and families and its increasingly downward pressure on families in the current climate affects the ways that educators engage families and, importantly, how they interact with schools. For example, anti-immigrant sentiment remains a pervasive narrative since the 2016 US presidential election. Educators working with immigrant multilingual children and families in schools were undoubtedly affected by public rhetoric and its effect on their undocumented children and families.

Immigration and Education: Experiences of Latino Families

For more than 11 million persons in the USA, the intersection of immigration and education policies has moved both in and out of the public spotlight over the past 10 years. Undocumented youth between the ages of 18 and 24, referred to in the USA as 'Dreamers', remain at the crossroad of state and federal policies. In fact, the US government's failure to provide a viable immigration policy that provides a legal pathway or that leads to permanent legal status to undocumented immigrants, continues to affect families and children in the USA. Lack of federal clarity regarding immigration and education policies for undocumented youth has incited fear and confusion among educators, families, counselors and community agencies across the country (Coady *et al.*, 2017). Recent news media (Mitchell, 2016) alerted educators that the new president would move swiftly to eliminate President Obama's 2012 executive order that established the Deferred Action for Childhood Arrivals (DACA; United States Citizenship and Immigration Services, 2017), invoking additional fear for children and families.

Strength for undocumented youth exists in large numbers. Jose Antonio Vargas, an undocumented journalist who was brought to the US from the Philippines as child, became a public figure and open activist in 2011 when he revealed that he, along with millions of other undocumented children, entered the USA with false documents. In 'My life as an undocumented immigrant', written for *The New York Times*, Vargas (2011) tells his story and its implications on his life. He writes,

> But I am still an undocumented immigrant. And that means living a different kind of reality. It means going about my day in fear of being found out. It means rarely trusting people, even those closest to me, with who I really am. It means keeping my family photos in a shoebox rather than displaying them on shelves in my home, so friends don't ask about them. It means reluctantly, even painfully, doing things I know are wrong and unlawful. And it has meant relying on a sort of 21st-century underground railroad of supporters, people who took an interest in my future and took risks for me.

Other narratives compete with Vargas's hopeful stance. These exist in daily media, across social media networks, are overheard in public spaces and in schools where immigrant children are educated. The broad macro-level narrative is one such system that affects the education of immigrant Latinos and families in the USA.

In 2013, I produced a film of one young Dreamer who was brought to the USA at the age of eight. Nancy graduated at the top of her high school class in a rural community. Her rich linguistic resources and strong family support structure competed with messages she received as a child and young woman about what she could not do in the USA. Nancy's story in *Waiting on DACA* (Deferred Action for Childhood Arrivals) (2013) is a similar one of hope but illuminates the reality of children like Nancy who live at the end of long dirt roads and remain out of sight in rural settings for fear of retribution and – most importantly to Nancy – the separation of families.

Attitudes toward immigrants frequently intersect with language ideologies in the USA. Negative attitudes toward languages other than English remain pervasive across the USA, despite the linguistic diversity in the country (Crawford, 2000). Speakers of languages other than English are too often deemed as inferior, when discourses such as 'can't speak English' and 'limited English' are labels used to refer to multilingual children and families. Some of those ideologies are fueled by myths and misconceptions about second language learning, namely that in order for children to develop English they must give up the first language. This myth has been repeatedly discredited by educational researchers (Cummins, 1979, 1981; Grosjean, 2010), yet the general public remains uninformed about the process of second language acquisition, literacy development and the contributions of multiple languages to cognition and learning. In sum, in today's linguistic climate, multilingualism is viewed as 'good for rich kids but bad for those who are poor' (Strauss, 2014: n.p.).

Zentella (2005) captures these stereotypes and narratives at length in her book on Latino families, *Building on Strength: Language and Literacy in Latino Families and Communities*. She writes how 'Spanish bashing' reinforces a powerless status among Latinos in the USA:

> Parents may try hard to encourage English and pass on Spanish along with their moral views about language, but they are not immune to attacks voiced in national debates about bilingual education and English-only laws, feelings of guilt about their lack of English, or blows delivered by their own children. Fortunately, some youngsters manage to resist Hispanophobic attitudes and policies ...and contest the oppressive policies that buttress dominant discourses. (Zentella, 2005: 9)

The statement quoted at the beginning of this chapter was made by a secondary rural school principal whose school consisted of a small but growing number of immigrant multilingual Latino youth. In the context of a conversation regarding the current social and political climate and its effect on learning, the principal noted that children were affected by the national negative rhetoric and discourse at the local level. He continued to describe the anxiety and fear that has become pervasive in those youths' lives, and the difficulty for them to feel safe when national anti-immigrant discourse, coupled with increasing local raids on rural businesses intended on 'rounding up' undocumented parents, particularly in rural settings with strong communities. We must ask how to interrogate those ideologies and how educators can build equity and justice – socially and economically? It is no wonder that families in rural settings who have mixed immigration statuses – where some family members may hold legal documents but others may not – elect to remain socially isolated and out of view, rather than to attend school functions and events, even when educators create welcoming environments. In essence, the macro system described above has a powerful influence on meso (school and family) and micro (child) systems.

Recent research on Latino parent engagement is noteworthy here because it continues to inform our work in two ways: first, the research findings underscore the same barriers to parental engagement that educators decry and say that they face; and secondly, the research is beginning to reveal some innovative and strategic ways that rural educators can build relationships with Latino families to support student learning, well-being and family engagement. However, as noted earlier in this volume, a list of strategies and welcoming school activities alone cannot ameliorate the impact of the grand narratives that adversely position immigrant Latinos in the USA.

Research on Rural Latino Family Engagement

Described earlier in this book, Jeynes's (2003) meta-analysis discusses how home communication among family members about education is a strong factor in the educational success of children across a variety of linguistic and racial backgrounds. For purposes of this chapter, I review additional recent research on Latino family engagement, particularly activities in rural settings, in order to synthesize 'what we know' about family engagement in the USA for Latino families who face repeated denigration by the media, politicians and anti-immigrant groups.

In my work with immigrant rural Latino families, I became initially interested in the linguistic resources that exist in the family home environment and how those literacies were appropriated by families, children and educators. In one study I conducted with a family whose children were both US and Mexican citizens, I had biweekly interactions with the parents and children over a 12-month period. The eldest son in the home was the same age as my own son, Thomas, and I frequently reflected upon the different access points to literacies that contrasted the two boys' school experiences. For example, my son had access to forms of literacies such as animé books, computer games and electronic devices. I believed that these were forms of literacies that supported an overall literacy 'repertoire' for my son, and my beliefs about literacy informed what I promoted in the home.

In contrast, the boy in my study had fewer traditional access points to the literacies that my son used. The family valued traditional books and the children had a home computer to use, but the computer did not have Internet access and it frequently did not work. When it was used, it was primarily for the children to type school reports and print at home, not for gaming or entertainment purposes. Other literacies, however, did characterize the home environment and were more linguistically rich than ours, because they reflected multiple languages and cultures. The parents in that study supported their children's use of books that exposed their own personal views and experiences of school literacy, namely that books were used for traditional learning. They wanted their children to acquire literacy for the purposes of a having a better future and some literacy practices (such as textbook reading) were prioritized over others (such as reading comic books). What I found, however, was that there were many written, oral and semiotic literacies that contributed to a multilingual household in both English, Spanish and Indigenous languages. It was, indeed, literacy-rich. Importantly, the family's Mexican background and religious traditions illuminated the family's identity, ontology and way of participating in and making sense of the world, epistemologically (Coady, 2009).

Other scholars of literacy development with Latino families have noted similar findings related to linguistic richness that contrast with grand narratives that diminish Latino families' knowledges and resources or funds of knowledge (Moll *et al.*, 1992). For example, Panferov (2010) interviewed two case study parents whose personal views of literacy framed their interactions with their children. She found that parents were intent and supportive of their children's literacy development. She noted that engaging parents as advocates in the home, where they interact most with their children, is more likely to support students' success in school.

Barone (2011) welcomed Latino families through a home literacy project that included shared reading. The project gave families strategies for building home and school-based literacies. The idea of 'sharing' was key to the success of the literacy project. Danzak (2011) found that for middle school English learner students, the opportunity to narrate their immigration experiences with graphic novels and comics was a successful way to support English language development and to tap in to multiple youth literacies. And in a study of an after school literacy program at a school comprised of 53% Latino students, Peercy *et al.*, (2013) noted how a community of practice (CoP) structure could be established with Latino families to support literacy development and to allow collaboration among families that did not exist during the school day. Latino parents appropriated school literacy practices into the home when they felt it would support the academic success of their child, a theme that bears repeating here.

Some studies findings emphasized the ways that Latino students' various home cultures can be translated into educational practices that bridge the cultural gap between the home and school environments. In rural Colorado, for example, Good *et al.* (2010) identified barriers to home–school relationships and recommended systematic planning and professional development among teachers to support families' school engagement. Protacio and Edwards (2015) found that a positive context of reception where families participated in a 'sharing time presentation' helped to bridge home culture with that of the school. Similarly, Zimmerman-Orozco (2011) noted a welcoming environment for 'Hispanic-American' immigrants. These dispositions toward immigrant Latino families are a departure point, but themselves not sufficient for sustained family engagement that counters the negative rhetoric toward families and children.

Based on the research reviewed here that has been conducted in the USA over the past decade, we can see that immigrant multilingual families in the USA demonstrate and support their children's education, language and literacy development in ways that are culturally appropriate to them and that reflect their own literacy experiences. They do so because they want their children to succeed. Unfortunately, there remain everyday barriers in education that detract from that goal: communicating in languages that parents do not understand, communicating about a child's education in ways that do not make sense to parents and not using family's ways of knowing to bridge cultural differences and beliefs about education.

Context of Rurality

How does rurality intersect with immigration for Latino families in terms of macro systemic discourses? Blankenship et al. (2016) note that both rural and urban settings have negative connotations; however, rural settings are 'often considered backwards, culturally scant, and lacking in sophistication' (Blankenship et al., 2016: 47). Yet rural settings can no longer remain on the fringe of politics and education. Kurtzleben (2016) describes the urban-rural voter divide that affected the outcome of the past US presidential election. She notes that the past decade has experienced a shift in voting patterns from Democratic to Republican candidates. In a similar vein, although rural schools have been largely overlooked across the educational landscape, scholars are noting the significant trends among children living in rural settings, their learning and the academic achievement of multilingual children.

Conclusion

The multiple effects of negative macro systemic discourses on immigrant, Latino families in rural settings is difficult to fully capture, but it is not surprising that the current sociopolitical context in the USA makes it more difficult for educators to engage rural families and to help them to feel safe and trusting. Family engagement in this context must reflect the reality of families' lived experiences, and knowledge of and response to the negative discourses and stereotypes of Latinos and immigrants. Informed, differentiated family engagement is possible through critical teacher reflection, *conscientizacao* and action in partnership with educators, advocates and community agencies in rural settings.

Activities

Activity 1

Write a list of words that you associate with immigrant in three minutes. View the film, *Waiting on DACA* (https://www.youtube.com/watch?v=ND TH1TJZHWo&feature=youtu.be). How did viewing the film change (or not) your ideas about undocumented immigrant youth in the US?

Activity 2

View the sequel film, *Long Journey to the American Dream* (https://www.youtube.com/watch?v=5XOpyrkaAyA). What is the American Dream for Nancy's father? How does this intersect with issues of immigration, rurality and poverty?

Activity 3

Relate Bronfenbrenner's ecological social systems theory model to your experiences in education. What systems seem to exert influence on your decision-making as an educator? How do large federal narratives of poverty, rurality and immigration appear to affect the education of immigrant Latino children in the USA?

Activity 4

How do you define American? Type your answer and follow the website. How did your refection change your view? See https://defineamerican.com/.

References

Blankenship, W.G., Reidel, M. and Sullivan, C.C. (2016) Teaching social studies to these students in this place: Exploring place in social studies teacher education In A.R. Crowe and A. Cuenca (eds) *Rethinking Social Studies Teacher Education in the Twenty-First Century* (pp. 41–60). Switzerland: Springer International.

Barone, D. (2011) Welcoming families: A parent literacy project in a linguistically rich, high-poverty school. *Early Childhood Education Journal* 38 (5), 377–384.

Bronfenbrenner, U. (1979) *The Ecology of Human Development: Experiments by Nature and Design.* Cambridge: Harvard University Press.

Bronfenbrenner, U. (1994) Ecological models of human development. In T. Husén and T.N. Postlethwaite (eds) *International Encyclopedia of Education* 3 (2), 1643–1647. New York: Elsevier Sciences.

Capps, R. Fix, M. and Jie Zong (2016) *A Profile of U.S. Children with Unauthorized Immigrant Parents.* Washington, DC: Migration Policy Institute.

Cicchinelli, L.F. and Beesley, A.D. (2017) Introduction: Current state of the science in rural education research. In G.C. Nugent, G.M. Kunz, S.M. Sheridan, T.A. Glover and L.L. Knoche (eds) *Rural Education Research in the United States* (pp. 1–14). Switzerland: Springer International.

Coady, M. (2009) '*Solamente libros importantes*': Literacy practices and ideologies of migrant farmworking families in north central Florida. In G. Li (ed.) *Multicultural Families, Home Literacies and Mainstream Schooling* (pp. 113–128). Charlotte, NC: New Age.

Coady, M. R., Heffington, D. and Marichal, N. (2017) Shifting sands in Florida: Rural perspectives on immigration, education, and undocumented youth under the incoming Trump administration. *Berkley Review in Education*. Conversations. See http://www.berkeleyreviewofeducation.com/cfc2016-blog/shifting-sands-in-florida-rural-perspectives-on-immigration-education-and-undocumented-youth-under-the-incoming-trump-administration

Crawford, J. (2000) *At War with Diversity: US Language Policy in an Age of Anxiety*. Clevedon: Multilingual Matters.

Cummins, J. (1979) Linguistic interdependence and the educational development of bilingual children. *Review of Educational Research* 49 (2), 222–251.

Cummins, J. (1981) The role of primary language development in promoting educational success for language minority students. In California State Department of Education (ed.) *Schooling and Language Minority Students: A Theoretical Rationale* (pp. 3–49). Los Angeles, CA: California State University.

Danzak, R.L. (2011) Defining identities through multiliteracies: EL teens narrate their immigration experiences as graphic stories. *Journal of Adolescent & Adult Literacy* 55 (3), 187–196.

Good, M.E., Masewicz, S. and Vogel, L. (2010) Latino English language learners: Bridging achievement and cultural gaps between schools and families. *Journal of Latinos and Education* 9 (4), 321–339.

Grosjean, F. (2010) *Bilingual: Life and Reality*. Cambridge, MA: Harvard University Press.

Hamman, L. (2018) Bilingualism for all? Interrogating language and equity in two-way immersion. Unpublished doctoral dissertation. University of Wisconsin, Madison.

Hansen-Thomas, H. (2018) Rural ESL: I only have two students! In J. Liontas (ed.) *The TESOL Encyclopedia of English Language Teaching*. Hoboken, NJ: Wiley & Sons.

Jeynes, W.H. (2003) A meta-analysis: The effects of parental involvement on minority children's academic achievement. *Education and Urban Society* 35 (2), 202–218.

Kurtzleben, D. (2013) Economists: Immigrants actually boost wages. *U.S. News & World Report*. See http://www.usnews.com/news/articles/2013/01/31/economists-immigrants-actually-boost-wages.

Kurtzleben, R. (2016) Rural voters played a big part in helping Trump defeat Clinton. *NPR Politics*. See https://www.npr.org/2016/11/14/501737150/rural-voters-played-a-big-part-in-helping-trump-defeat-clinton.

Lemke, J.L. (2000) Across the sales of time: Artifacts, activities and meanings in ecosocial systems. *Mind, Culture, and Activity* 7 (4), 273–290.

Mitchell, C. (2016) Trump vows to 'work something out' for DREAMers, but offers no details on plan. The Language Learning blog, *Education Week*. See http://blogs.edweek.org/edweek/learning-the-language/2016/12/trump_were_going_to_work_somet.html

Moll, L.C., Amanti, C., Neff, D. and Gonzalez, N. (1992) Funds of knowledge for teaching: Using a qualitative approach to connect homes and classrooms. *Theory Into Practice* 31, 132–141.

National Center for Education Statistics (2017) Fast facts on English language learners. See https://nces.ed.gov/fastfacts/display.asp?id=96.

National Public Radio (NPR) (2016) Why America's schools have a money problem. *Morning Edition*. See https://www.npr.org/2016/04/18/474256366/why-americas-schools-have-a-money-problem.

Panferov, S. (2010) Increasing ELL parental involvement in our schools: Learning from the parents. *Theory Into Practice* 49 (2), 106–112.

Passel, J.S. and Cohn, D. (2016) Unauthorized immigrant totals rise in 7 states, fall in 14. *Pew Research Center, Hispanic Trends*. See http://www.pewhispanic.org/2014/11/18/unauthorized-immigrant-totals-rise-in-7-states-fall-in-14/.

Peercy, M.M., Martin-Beltran, M. and Daniel, S.M. (2013) Learning together: Creating a community of practice to support English language learner literacy. *Language, Culture and Curriculum* 26 (3), 284–299.

Protacio, M.S. and Edwards, P.A. (2015) Restructuring sharing time for English learners and their parents. *The Reading Teacher* 68 (6), 413–421.

Strange, M., Johnson, J., Showalter, D. and Klein, R. (2012) Why rural matters 2011–2012: The condition of rural education in the 50 states. *A Report of the Rural School and Community Trust Policy Program*. See https://www.nwp.org/cs/public/print/resource/3771.

Strauss, V. (2014) Why is bilingual education good for rich kids but bad for poor immigrant students? *The Washington Post*. See https://www.washingtonpost.com/news/answer-sheet/wp/2014/10/24/why-is-bilingual-education-good-for-rich-kids-but-bad-for-poor-immigrant-students/?utm_term=.a296b1f25cc3

Suárez-Orozco, C., Onaga, M. and Lardemelle, C. (2010) Promoting academic engagement among immigrant adolescents through school-family-community collaboration. *Professional School Counseling* 14 (1), 15–26.

Suro, R. and Singer, A. (2002) Latino growth in metropolitan America: Changing patterns, new locations. Center on Urban & Metropolitan Policy and the Pew Hispanic Center. Washington, DC. See https://www.brookings.edu/wp-content/uploads/2016/06/surosinger.pdf

United States Citizenship and Immigration Services (2017) DACA. See https://www.uscis.gov/archive/consideration-deferred-action-childhood-arrivals-daca.

Vargas, J.A. (2011) My life as an undocumented immigrant. *The New York Times*. See http://www.nytimes.com/2011/06/26/magazine/my-life-as-an-undocumented-immigrant.html.

Zentella, A.M. (2005) *Building on Strength: Language and Literacy in Latino Families and Communities*. New York: Teachers College Press.

Zimmerman-Orozco, S. (2011) A circle of caring. *Educational Leadership* 68 (8), 64–68.

7 The Role of Community Agencies in Family Engagement

with Robin Lewy and Fran Ricardo
The Rural Women's Health Project

Highlights

- Scenario connecting community agencies and schools.
- The role of community agencies in rural settings.
- An ecology of services for rural multilingual families.
- Suggestions for educators.
- Activities for further learning.

Real Scenario

An elementary teacher is concerned about her student, María. She is a six-year-old girl who has recently arrived from El Salvador. María is quiet, rarely smiles and is very obedient. She seems tired all of the time and does not interact well with other children. Her mother is sweet and timid, but María does not present as being particularly bonded with her mother.

What steps should the school guidance counselors, staff and teachers take to respond to the teacher's concerns? What is the role of community agencies in supporting María and her mother?

Introduction

Multilingual families who do not speak the language of the school staff and teachers can feel uncomfortable interacting with their children's teachers and administrators due to cultural and linguistic differences, and their level of ease in communicating is difficult to ascertain. Often, infrequent interactions between schools and families impede the opportunity to include families in educational decisions for their children. In addition, rural multilingual families may feel excluded, intimidated, powerless and voiceless in educational decisions. Community agencies play an integral role as 'voices' and advocates for rural multilingual families and they can act as key partners with schools and families to bridge families' needs for social, health and related services and the services that schools can or do offer.

In this chapter, we consider multilingual family engagement from the perspective of the community agency, which offers a different 'lens' through which families' experiences can be viewed. This chapter has three main goals. First, we describe community agencies, who they are and what they do, using our own experience as partners and health advocates for rural multilingual families. Secondly, we discuss the role of community agencies as resources for both schools and families with a focus on how community agencies can fill gaps in communication as interpreters and cultural brokers. Included are several ways that community agencies can assist and partner with guidance counselors and support rural multilingual families with comprehensive services by networking within rural settings. Finally, suggestions are also offered for educators. Key to this chapter is understanding various family needs, illuminating the strengths of families, and how to identify and provide targeted support for the child's and family's well-being.

What are Community Agencies?

Community agencies, often referred to as community-based organizations, are entities – frequently nonprofit organizations – that are located in and provide services to communities. Community agencies vary in terms of mission and focus. Rural community agencies, which focus on addressing the extensive individual and family needs in communities where resources are limited and the distance between resources is great, can be helpful in resolving multilingual families' tangible needs, such as access to food, rent assistance, prescription discounts, and medical and dental care. However, agencies that focus on the internal barriers faced by immigrants, such as language and cultural differences, often have the opportunity to get to know the families and interact with them in their home languages. Such intimate interactions, grounded in building trusting relationships, often offer families the opportunity to ask for clarification about experiences they have had within the school system and its corresponding school culture.

The Rural Women's Health Project (RWHP), is a nonprofit health justice organization located in rural north central Florida. Our mission is to work with rural communities to overcome their health barriers. With over 25 years of experience working with immigrant communities, we envision health as the broad spectrum of emotional and physical wellness. The RWHP designs and implements community-based health education projects, promotes lay health worker efforts and develops community-driven materials to assist communities in strengthening their understanding of critical health and community issues. Our approach focuses on leadership and community development, working in tandem with health clinics, farmworker organizations, schools and immigrant policy initiatives. Through this work, we have assisted families by leading health campaigns, accessing health, education and legal services, and see this work as essential to supporting multilingual families in schools.

For schools seeking to support children and families, it is important to first acknowledge that multilingual families are not monolithic. In Guatemala alone there are 23 official languages and across Latin America's approximate 650 million people, more than 1000 languages are used (Noack & Gamio, 2015). Stereotyping and grouping of families by country of origin only reveals common cultural elements. For refugees or economic migrants, each family's journey has been unique. When an unaccompanied minor crosses three borders to arrive in the USA, they have experienced a unique reality when compared to a Venezuelan child flying into the USA and then seeking asylum. A child who has lived in a refugee camp for three years after fleeing bombing in Syria will have their own set of trauma and recovery. Breaking away from war, poverty, repression, natural disasters and premigration experiences, leads people to calmer ground. General commonalities are often reflected through their future goals and dreams, often summed up in Spanish as 'para salir adelante' (to move forward with one's life). Schools that experience an influx of immigrants, or over the years have seen a steady increase, need to be both prepared with special services to receive multilingual students and respond to the needs of families. These two factors are the springboard for the successful academic performance of multilingual children.

With this in mind, some of the work we do includes acting as linguistic interpreters and cultural brokers in rural school settings, working with guidance counselors to provide targeted relief and support in times of crisis, and aligning a broad range of services for rural multilingual families.

Community Agencies and an Ecology of Services for Rural Multilingual Families

The Rural Women's Health Project's framework for engaging rural immigrant families is an ecological model of services (see Figure 7.1). We begin with the concept of the individual at the center – the heart – of the model. The individual can be the adult or a child. For example, a monolingual immigrant child initially arrives at school with embedded experiences that began in their home country. These experiences are compounded for most by the trauma of migration as seen in the second outer band (including fear, insecurity, debt, reduced self-esteem, etc.). For instance, we have found that children who migrate from areas of conflict, or through areas of conflict, face fear, insecurity and isolation. Those feelings can be compounded by acts of violence and exploitation that they experienced on the

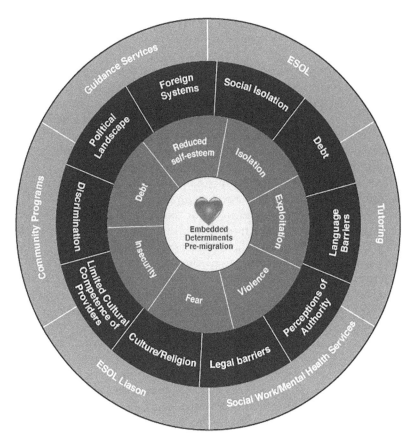

Figure 7.1 Ecology of the challenges and barriers to social services for rural mono-lingual families

Notes: Inner band, immigrants and the embedded determinants brought to the new country; second band, new determinants that impact adaptation, emotional health and capacity; third band, systemic barriers to immigrants' accessing services; outer band, services often available for immigrant student success in the USA

Source: Rural Women's Health Project © 2018, Rural Women's Health Project. rwhp.org

journey of migration. Clearly, emotional health concerns, such as those that María (from the opening scenario) may be facing, present in school settings where children spend a significant amount of time.

If we look at María's story within the ecological framework we can see the challenges that her family will face in accessing services. We need to understand that María had not lived with her mother since infancy. She traveled with her grandmother, who she had always lived with, to be reunited with her mother in the USA. At the border she was forcibly separated from her grandmother by border agents and was subsequently deported. María was finally reunited with her mother weeks later, after having lived in a detention facility. She was emotionally affected by having been separated from the woman who had always been her emotional base. And, then she was reunited with her mother, who she had previously only known from phone calls. Trauma has marked much of María's path. Support, space and patience need to be part of her academic reality.

Surrounding the second outer band of the circle, are barriers that families face in accessing community agencies and social support in a rural community, the third outer band. Some of those factors include families' debt, language, cultural and religious differences, the foreign nature of the services being provided, systemic bureaucracy, the fear embedded of authority figures and families' perceptions of authority, social isolation of families and the political landscape that shapes whether or not multilingual families feel welcomed in rural communities.

Finally, at the outermost band of our ecological social services framework are multiple services that immigrant multilingual families and children could access to resolve their challenges. Most will require support from the school and community agencies to locate. As noted throughout this book, in rural settings, a main challenge is ensuring access to social services so that students and families can adjust to their new community and thrive. We have found six support structures that educators and guidance counselors can access when engaging rural multilingual families and students. Guidance services, second language (English to speakers of other languages, ESOL) services, tutoring, community programs, mental health services and school–home (ESOL) liaisons are some of those.

In our experience, gaining parental and family acceptance of community social services can be a challenge for two reasons. First, immigrant multilingual families who migrate into new and rural communities are unaware of social services or these systems and frequently feel that they should not access social services, and with good reason. Currently, in the USA, use of these services could have a negative impact on immigrants' legal status or future acquisition of permanent residency or citizenship. We have also learned that many immigrant families do not want to 'burden' teachers and schools in identifying services to resolve needs. Schools are often seen as sites solely for education. The most common reason for hesitation in accessing social services is that multilingual families, who do not speak the language of the community, face language and cultural barriers that make it difficult to communicate their needs. Therefore, community agencies, who build trusting relationships with families, can be critical partners in identifying services, working with families to communicate their needs and accepting services to help them transition into rural communities.

The Role of Community Agencies as Interpreters and Cultural Brokers

It is clear that multilingual families face endemic realities found in many rural areas across the world: economic challenges, and cultural and religious traditions that guide family life. Educational status and experiences also vary. But, we must not forget that the prior cultural experiences with the educational systems from families' home countries play a significant role in the way in which parents will interpret their childreńs experiences in a new country. For example, in many parts of the world, parental interaction with the school is uncommon. When this is the experience of a parent, attendance at the new school's parent–teacher meetings, participation as chaperones for outings or contributions to school activities may not be understood and may not occur.

In one small rural community where we worked, there was a high level of participation by parents at teacher–parent conferences. However, the vice principal of the school noticed that the multilingual parents' presence was more limited. Unsure why, she turned to a friend at a local community agency that provided afterschool care to many of the students. Being able to communicate in the language of the families and understand their cultural background, the friend soon learned some of the barriers to multilingual parent attendance at conferences: the school's English-only flyers announcing the event, a lack of clarity of expectations of what the parent's role is at the meeting and the teacher's presentations of child test scores were unclear to those unfamiliar with school assessments. To remedy these issues, the school reached out to the local college's International Student Clubs for assistance. The principal found willing volunteers to develop clear informational flyers in the languages of the multilingual students' families and to assist with translation at scheduled at parent–teacher conferences.

In our work, we have found that immigrant parents might not approach the school to address poor student performance, bullying or other issues. Not approaching the school might be interpreted by the administration as parents' disinterest or negligence. In fact, this misinterpretation comes from the misunderstanding that multilingual families may have been traditionally accustomed to leaving those issues for the school to manage. Therefore, the mere translation of invitations, letters and announcements *cannot* always bridge the communication divide. Understanding school culture requires a clear articulation of school style along with parental and student expectations from the start. This is important to counteract the parent's previous experiences of interacting with their children's education in their home country.

There are different perspectives on the best way for multilingual children to acquire language (see Gass, 2014); however, language acquisition at the expense of healthy home communication is an unfavorable strategy. Multilingual parents, who are committed to their child's quick language success in their new community language acquisition, can be fearful of the loss of cultural identification and weakened communication between parents and their children. Community partners can play an important role in supporting family communication and in maintaining a parent–child equilibrium. Whether programs serve families in their primary language or not, programs that value families' home culture are great partners in encouraging both parents and children to embrace family communication in the home language as well as the school language as a tool to move ahead.

The maintenance of home language should not be underestimated. Communication challenges in immigrant multilingual families become exacerbated when, for example, children acquire the language of school at a faster rate than their parents. This becomes a barrier to family harmony, especially with teenaged children. It must remain a right for parents to preserve the home language and culture while acquiring the language of schooling.

Working with Guidance Counselors in Times of Crisis

Community agencies can also play a unique role in supporting guidance counselors at times of crisis within rural communities. In addition to offering linguistic support, gaining insight into family functioning and acting as cultural brokers, community agencies can partner with each other to ensure that rural multilingual families are safe. A short story illustrates this point. On a fall, Tuesday afternoon, a local meat-packing factory in a rural town was raided by Immigration and Customs Enforcement (ICE) in the USA. Hysterical calls flooded the school's offices and older children's cell phones. Immigrant rural families anxiously tried to share messages of love as authorities began to approach the factory to 'round up', question and detain undocumented people. Sixty immigrant parents were arrested. Classrooms erupted with children crying and trying to leave school property to find their parents or to provide care to younger siblings. Panic among school administration also mounted as to how to respond to the situation. Hours later, over 60 parents were in detention and 113 children were left without one or both parents. Teachers and school administration were left trying to find caregivers, listed on students' emergency cards, to pick up children, and to provide food and shelter for the children that governmental child welfare agencies could not place. The teachers and school administrators were also worried about the next school day. Relief to the school came by the guidance counselors calling and reaching out to local churches serving immigrant populations and area food banks. Without these agency partners, children would have been left without the comfort necessary to respond to this local crisis.

In the story above, the school guidance counselors managed to identify support with community agencies for food, shelter, mental health support and transportation. Churches were one organization that provided immediate relief and area food banks worked in concert with local families. In this case, multiple community agencies needed to quickly come together and align with schools. However, without already having established a relationship with community agencies, the schools would have been unable to support the children and families during this crisis. Other scenes reflect a similar need for guidance counselors – or an educator who works in a similar capacity to provide social support to students – to know and understand local community services for rural multilingual families. Weather-related disasters, the death of loved ones, issues of migration, trauma, strife abroad and loss are some other events that negatively affect all rural children. Community agencies that know the linguistic and cultural backgrounds of students and families can be a critical support mechanism during crises.

The Role of Community Agencies Aligning Services for Rural Multilingual Families

A third area in which community agencies can support rural multilingual families in schools is through the networks that they have access to in order to align a wider range of services. For instance, one contribution of community agencies to schools is in establishing a comprehensive system of support that includes mental and physical health, dental care, food and clothing. Community agencies can tap into a network of providers that rural multilingual families, particularly those new to a rural community, are unaware of.

In a rural, north Florida town where immigrants work in agriculture and take care of race horses, long work days are the norm. Just this reality alone impedes access to health services by many rural immigrant parents. This problem came to light when the father of a student working on a local horse farm suffered diabetic shock as a result of uncontrolled diabetes. The oldest son was pulled out of his high school science class in order to translate at the local area hospital. When the oldest son's high school teacher visited the hospital after school, he learned that families were not accessing medical care except when there were injuries. Turning for guidance to a local health education program offered by a community agency, the teacher and school collaborated in hosting a preventive health fair that included a broad spectrum of health care screening opportunities, such as high blood pressure, diabetes and domestic violence. Offering services in the evening, around the work schedule of many of the immigrant parents, resulted in a huge turnout of parents seeking healthcare. With planning, the event became an opportunity for the children to participate in a workshop about medical professions hosted simultaneously.

Rethinking schools as a community center, especially in rural areas, can transform the way in which families see the school and their new community. This 'community center' approach can be as simple as a once-yearly health fair as described above. Thinking beyond the school system can potentially have a multiplying effect on rural multilingual family engagement. By simply bringing partners to the school, new connections and trust are facilitated; families will see these players as trusting agencies that are approachable. The families are also now aware of the services each partner plays, increasing their integration into their new community and into services systems.

Likewise, guiding families to local sites where children can interact can mitigate families' sense of isolation and apprehension in engaging beyond school events. Engagement outside of schools can help to build confidence. Helping to see that this occurs can be best accomplished by inviting community programs and services into the schools to present programs to children or at events where they can actively promote their services. Again, using the school as the staging ground is beneficial to winning the confidence of multilingual families for the services offered. This might include exposure to library services or community parks and programs, communities of faith, or physical or creative activities and community events such as fall harvest fairs. Encouraging families' exploration of area options also strengthens family learning and allows parents to model both social interaction challenges and successes in front of their children. It might also help to overcome hesitation to engagement, as a result of issues of cultural and language differences, common among immigrant families. This will also serve to support the concepts of unified family and community efforts.

Recommendations for Educators Working with Rural Multilingual Families

Between 2016 and 2019, we worked as a community agency partner in rural schools with multilingual families. On school sites, we have collaborated with school administrators, teachers and guidance counselors to serve as language interpreters and cultural brokers, mediate written family–school communication, situate a referral service for families to use in order to identify social and healthcare services for immigrant multilingual families, and to guide families to an array of legal services. Because families have interacted with and have come to trust us, they have described to us the barriers that they face in terms engaging with schools and learning how to access support services. Below we offer suggestions for educators and administrators based on our work as a community agency and partner.

(1) Create meetings of opportunity, instead of concern. Bring in families when things are going well, not just when there is a problem or concern for a child's academic challenges or behavior. Given the challenges of distance, time, and the need for families to work, engaging rural multilingual families should be fruitful and offer solutions or linkage to opportunities for families (such as afterschool programs, clubs for children to join, etc.).

(2) Immigrant families are often hesitant to offer information or to ask directly for services. The use of direct questions can be seen as culturally insensitive or intrusive. 'What do you want to ask me about your child's progress', could better be replaced with 'I am happy with your son's progress, especially as he is learning our language. Maybe you can give me some ideas of what I can do to assist him and your family.' Finding ways to express your willingness to assist families includes both expressing success and as stated above, opportunities.

(3) Use professional translation and interpretation and do not depend on parents' understanding 'a little' English or on children for communication. We have repeatedly noted that even in parent–teacher meetings when teachers do not believe that families need an interpreter, because they know 'a little' English, families have not accurately understood the content of the meeting and what schools expect from them. The same holds true for translations of complex and technical school documents. Verbal and written communication needs to be not just translated, but interpreted to meet literacy levels and cultural relevancy for families.

(4) Do not assume that barriers or experiences are the same for all immigrants. Differentiated family engagement is crucial for rural multilingual families. Even when families seem to speak the same language, their experiences, backgrounds and mode of migration vary tremendously.

(5) Preface your meetings with words of support and compassion. Learning and using families' home languages to greet them is one way to demonstrate your interest in their culture and openness to making respectful connections.

(6) Explain the services that you are recommending slowly and without acronyms. Families will respond when they understand; however, much of the school–home communication between teachers and families is lost in school and academic acronyms.

Conclusion

The apprehension felt by both schools and newly arrived multilingual families can hinder an efficient and welcoming start for multilingual students and their families. Strategizing approaches to reduce the obstacles resulting from expectations and apprehension does not need to be the sole responsibility of the family, teacher or school. Building a community for immigrant families benefits from the involvement of partners. Extending the responsibility to a larger group of community agencies and members is a realistic way to systemically respond to creating a conducive educational environment for multilingual students to excel and a safe space for their parents to engage.

Partnering with community agencies can lighten the load on the school as they can serve as a beacon, which sheds light that can enhance communication and understanding. It allows space for the insertion of new cultures and the respecting of the uniqueness of each immigrant family's story. Diminishing these barriers is integral to the ultimate academic success of children.

We need to recognize that many immigrant children will have a hard time acclimating to even the kindest school environment or community. There needs to be both recognition and space for children and their families to work through premigratory realities that we might never understand or hear about. Emotional and academic development may be stymied if we do not stay conscious of the broader spectrum of experiences that might hinder academic achievement.

Evaluate your and your school's true capacity to meet the needs of rural multilingual learners and their families. Recognize that the effort placed on identifying and creating alliances with community services is your closest link to a potential lifeline in meeting the spectrum of needs that will face the families you serve. Building respect and space for agency inclusion in your school can be the source of a partnership that can create a trio of support of multilingual children, their parents and the school home.

Activities

Activity 1

Identify four social service agencies in your local community that could support rural multilingual families. Ensure that at least one works in the area of health and mental health services, and one can address food insecurity or clothing and housing. What are their names? What is their mission? What is their contact information? Call the agencies directly and identify the language(s) in which their services are offered, the days in which multilingual staff answer phones and when they are physically on-site.

Activity 2

Using the information above, design a local resource guide in multiple languages that you can use (a) with school office staff and (b) with rural multilingual families.

References

Gass, S. (2014) *Second Language Acquisition: An Introductory Course* (4th edn). New York: Routledge.
Noack, R. and Gamio, L. (2015) The world's languages in 7 maps and charts. *The Washington Post*. See https://www.washingtonpost.com/news/worldviews/wp/2015/04/23/the-worlds-languages-in-7-maps-and-charts/?noredirect=on&utm_term=.3251598b0320.

8 Conclusions for 21st Century Rural, Multilingual Family Engagement

Introduction

Earlier in this book, I described the dearth of research and the absence of a fluid, dynamic, knowledge-base on home–school relationships from a non-Western perspective. Recent research conducted in China, in fact, indicates that, in contrast to US-based middle- and upper-middle class parents, low income parents in China are more likely to be involved in their child's education (Kim *et al.*, 2017). Kim and colleagues' work was conducted in urban settings, however. We know even less about parental engagement in rural settings, and it would not be surprising to learn about variations in beliefs about, and experiences in, education across other international venues.

At the beginning of this book, I also noted the urgent need to complicate and understand rural settings, particularly the ways that they function and the social processes occurring within them, rather than reifying and reproducing stereotypes about rural educators, students, and families. Against a backdrop of digging deeper into social processes, social networks and community functioning, differentiating family engagement becomes illuminated. In other words, until we reject fossilized concepts of family engagement, as well as static concepts of families and multilingualism, we cannot progress toward humanizing practices that truly make a difference in education. In addition, rather than typifying or essentializing people in physical settings as 'rural' in which images of poverty, violence (Vance, 2016) and isolation rush forward, educators need to unravel rurality for what it represents on its own, outside of a false urban-rural duality, which Reynolds (2017: xxi) states simply, 'is not correct'.

At the same time, however, I am reminded of my work with K-12 educators in a small, rural community. Beginning in 2016, I have engaged in an educator professional development project under Project STELLAR (Supporting Teachers of English Language Learners Across Rural settings) with a rural school district partner in Florida. The educators are teachers, principals, reading coaches and guidance counselors. The aim of the work has been to prepare educators for rural multilingual students, and a large and significant component of this work has been in building relational trust with rural multilingual families. When I began the work, it was clear that despite the fact that educators readily acknowledged their geospatial setting as 'rural', they continued to gauge their success, work and identity against an invisible nonrural image. In other words, although they were rural educators and knew what that meant to them, they located their own identities in contrast to urbanized settings, a nearby small city in fact, which seemed richer, more sophisticated and academically successful. The nearby small city did not appear to have any of the same problems that my rural school district did: teachers in the small city were paid more and had more curricular and material resources, schools experienced lower teacher turnover and families seemed more 'engaged'. The benchmark for my rural partner school district, then, was the image of urbanity or something close to it.

Once the project was underway, the teacher and educators in Project STELLAR participated in a course called *Teaching in High Poverty Rural Settings*. The course existed previously without the 'rurality' component – it was formerly called *Teaching in High Poverty Settings* – but we modified the course by examining rurality and by reducing the amount of academic text while introducing narrative text. The text narratives, which were personal stories of immigrants from different languages and cultural backgrounds, cut across reading ability levels (some of the books were youth or children's literature) and genre. The aim of the course materials was to build empathy among the educators for rural immigrants, students and multilingual families and tie those to school-based strategies that specifically included family engagement.

It was about that time that I started reflecting more deeply on the label 'rural' even though I had been working with the district for about 10 years. Academics like myself decry the label as essentializing, stereotyping and reifying ideologies that are false and binary. But I also witnessed the educators in my project develop more agency around the term and question their assumptions regarding the theoretically more successful school district nearby. When they began – we began – to examine more carefully the way that the community functioned, the contributions of multilingual families, how schools were financed based on property taxes and the reduced tax base derived from agricultural farmland, we started to see our work differently. They seemed to feel differently. The pressure for students to meet state standards of academic achievement persisted, but we recognized that the story was more complicated than that. The educators in Project STELLAR started to 'own' the term rural and this recognition seemed to empower them. The more we understood how the work we were doing was unique across the USA, the more urgent it became and the more empowered the educators seemed to feel. In other words, once the benchmark of an invisible urban binary was removed, the educators seemed freer to examine the way that their own school district functioned, who multilingual families were and what they needed. There was still pressure for families to come to the school for Parent Leadership Committee meetings, a biannual state-required event, but many changes began to take place beyond that requirement. Some changes included different expectations of families such as the frequency of in-school presence and more targeted communication in families' home languages.

The participants in the project began to make educational decisions that met the needs of students in their specific schools, situated within their rural school district and without outside help. They looked for additional resources from within the community and with community agencies; they read about alternative types of language programs; and in a dramatic shift, one school decided to place their *best* teacher with the lowest-performing multilingual students in a 4th grade self-contained English language learner classroom. Almost immediately, we noticed changes to student participation in class, the use of students' first languages as learning resources, and the cultural and identity affirmation of rural multilingual students.

In addition to the educational changes made in the district, the educators remained committed to the project. No one dropped out of the program. Rather, almost all of them indicated that they wished to apply to graduate school to earn their next advanced degree. And this is what I believe reflects the essence of rural educators: commitment to their communities, perseverance and resourcefulness, or as Casey Tieken (2014: 153) well articulates,

> it's the school that fosters these elements of this sense of community. In the school, relationships are built and maintained, alumni stay in touch with one another, parents talk with teachers, children see their cousins; here, community members adopt the identity that marks them as belonging.

All of this is a long way of saying that while there are problems with labelling such as rural, it is not the labels that are problematic but rather what we do with them. In the case of my partner district, the label bestowed a sense of empowerment, or so it appeared to me.

Setting an Agenda and a Call for Change

Scholars and educators need a much clearer and deeper understanding of rural multilingual families' beliefs and experiences in education across varied settings around the world. They need less static views of families and fewer fossilized instructional and educational practices to engage families. This work is in its infancy, but I am hopeful that scholars of education will continue to expand their work to include topics such as: rich qualitative descriptions of rurality worldwide; the nature of literacy, languages and multilingualism across rural settings; diverse cultural practices among various configurations of 'families' worldwide; and a broader understanding of poverty issues and their effect on schools and multilingual families in rural settings. I also truly hope that schools will throw away 'to do' lists with multilingual families and, instead, examine the way their communities function, who families are and how they can build relational trust with them. Issues of human migration will continue to have an impact on rural schools and there an urgency in equipping educators for diversity.

This book, perhaps ambitious in its orientation, aimed to build a framework for examining rural multilingual family engagement, the multiple ecological systems that affect educators and families in rural settings, and the alignment of those to dynamic instructional and educational practices that engage families. Like the diversity within and across rural settings themselves, this book's vision is to equip educators to engage families in unique, differentiated ways that build relational trust and care. There is no doubt that the starting point for this work is teachers and educators as learners themselves, whose knowledge, experiences, beliefs and attitudes toward multilingual students and families interweave as they make educational decisions in classrooms and schools. Grounded in the theories of critical consciousness and linguistically-responsive pedagogy, the book seeks to equip readers with tools to reflect and act on behalf of families and in the spirit of praxis and social change.

In today's international sociopolitical climate, we are at a crossroads on several educational fronts: first, we need better preparation for teachers and leaders in rural, diverse multilingual school settings with targeted professional development for educators in those settings. Several critically important topics can no longer be ignored: understanding of immigration and human migration and its effect at the student, family and school levels; school funding sources for rural schools and the urgency of illuminating inequities in funding based on property taxes that further depress rural communities; barriers to accessing human resources; and advocacy to rupture oppressive and inequitable social and economic structures on behalf of rural multilingual families. Casey Tieken (2014: 190) suggests that 'we can develop a more nuanced and connected approach to education policy, writing reforms that balance individual and collective needs, support local and national goals, foster racial and geographic justice'. I welcome exciting educational conversations and change across linguistically diverse contexts to advance our work with rural multilingual families locally and globally.

References

Casey Tieken, M. (2014) *Why Rural Schools Matter.* Chapel Hill, NC: University of North Carolina Press.

Kim, S.W., Brown, K., Kim, E.J. and Fong, V.L. (2017) 'Poorer children study better': How urban Chinese young adults perceive relationships between wealth and academic achievement. *Comparative Education Review* 62 (1), 84–102.

Reynolds, W. (2017) *Forgotten Places: Critical Studies in Rural Education.* New York: Peter Lang.

Vance, J.D. (2016) *Hillbilly Elegy: A Memoir of a Family and Culture in Crisis.* New York: Harper.

Index

CPSIA information can be obtained
at www.ICGtesting.com
Printed in the USA
LVHW081549200122
709000LV00010B/749

9 781788 923255